American Civil War
Primary Sources

American Civil War
Primary Sources

**Kevin Hillstrom
and
Laurie Collier
Hillstrom**
Lawrence W. Baker, Editor

U·X·L®

AN IMPRINT OF THE GALE GROUP

DETROIT · SAN FRANCISCO · LONDON
BOSTON · WOODBRIDGE, CT

American Civil War: Primary Sources

Kevin Hillstrom and Laurie Collier Hillstrom

Staff

Lawrence W. Baker, *U•X•L Senior Editor*
Carol DeKane Nagel, *U•X•L Managing Editor*
Tom Romig, *U•X•L Publisher*

Rita Wimberley, *Senior Buyer*
Evi Seoud, *Assistant Production Manager*
Dorothy Maki, *Manufacturing Manager*
Mary Beth Trimper, *Production Director*

Michelle DiMercurio, *Art Director*
Cynthia Baldwin, *Product Design Manager*

Shalice Shah-Caldwell, *Permissions Specialist*
Pamela Reed, *Imaging Coordinator*
Leitha Etheridge-Sims, *Cataloger*
Robert Duncan, *Senior Imaging Specialist*
Michael Logusz, *Imaging Specialist*
Randy A. Bassett, *Image Database Supervisor*
Barbara J. Yarrow, *Imaging and Multimedia Content Manager*

Marco Di Vita, Graphix Group, *Typesetting*

Library of Congress Cataloging-in-Publication Data

Hillstrom, Kevin, 1963–
    American Civil War. Primary sources / Kevin Hillstrom and Laurie Collier
Hillstrom ; Lawrence W. Baker, editor.
        p. cm.
    Includes bibliographical references and index.
    ISBN 0-7876-3824-2
        1. United States—History—Civil War, 1861–1865–Sources—Juvenile liter-
ature. I. Hillstrom, Laurie Collier, 1965– II. Baker, Lawrence W. III. Title.
    E464.H55 1999
    973.7—dc21   99-046919

Cover photographs reproduced courtesy of the Library of Congress and
the National Archives and Records Administration.

Copyright © 2000
U•X•L, an imprint of The Gale Group
27500 Drake Road
Farmington Hills, MI 48331-3535

Printed in the United States of America

10 9 8 7 6 5 4 3

Contents

Advisory Board

S pecial thanks are due to U•X•L's Civil War Reference Library advisors for their invaluable comments and suggestions:

- Deborah Hammer, Former Librarian, Queens Borough Public Library, Jamaica, New York
- Ann Marie LaPrise, Librarian, Detroit Public Library, Elmwood Park Branch, Detroit, Michigan
- Susan Richards, Media Specialist, Northwest Junior High School, Coralville, Iowa

Reader's Guide

American Civil War: Primary Sources presents fourteen full or excerpted documents written by people who participated in the events of the Civil War. These documents range from notable speeches that mark important points in the conflict to personal diaries and letters that reflect the hopes, dreams, fears, and experiences of ordinary soldiers and civilians of the era. Some of the selections discuss highly personal issues, such as the terror of being in combat. Others chronicle events that fundamentally altered the course of the Civil War, like President Abraham Lincoln's Emancipation Proclamation and the letters between Union general William T. Sherman and Atlanta, Georgia, city leaders, relating to the 1864 fall of Atlanta. Further, the works included in this volume present a wide range of perspectives on the conflict. Some entries provide insights into the feelings of men and women who were devoted to the Confederacy, for example, while others provide a glimpse into the motivations of equally dedicated Union loyalists.

Each excerpt presented in *American Civil War: Primary Sources* includes the following additional material:

- An **introduction** places the document and its author in a historical context.

- **"Things to remember while reading..."** offers readers important background information and directs them to central ideas in the text.

- **"What happened next..."** provides an account of subsequent events, both in the war and in the life of the author.

- **"Did you know..."** provides significant and interesting facts about the document, the author, or the events discussed.

- **"For further reading"** lists sources for more information on the author, the topic, or the document.

Other features of *American Civil War: Primary Sources* include short biographies of featured authors, photographs and illustrations depicting the personalities and events discussed in the documents, and sidebars presenting additional information on unusual or significant aspects of the issue or event under discussion. In addition, a glossary runs alongside each primary document that defines unfamiliar terms and ideas contained in the material. Finally, *American Civil War: Primary Sources* provides an "American Civil War Timeline" that lists significant dates and events of the Civil War era and a cumulative subject index.

American Civil War Reference Library

American Civil War: Primary Sources is only one component of a three-part American Civil War Reference Library. The other two titles in this multivolume set are:

- *American Civil War: Almanac:* This work presents a comprehensive overview of the Civil War. The volume's fourteen chapters cover all aspects of the conflict, from the prewar issues and events that divided the nation to the war itself—an epic struggle from 1861 to 1865 that changed the political and social landscape of America forever. The chapters are arranged chronologically and explore such topics as the events leading up to the war, slavery, Europe's view of the war, the secession of Southern states, various Civil War battles, and Reconstruction. Also included are two chapters that cover two unique groups during the Civil War: women and blacks. The *Almanac* also contains over ninety photographs and maps, "Words to Know" and "People to Know" sections, a timeline, and an index.

- *American Civil War: Biographies:* This two-volume set presents profiles of sixty important figures from the Civil War era. The essays cover such key people as politicians Abraham Lincoln and Jefferson Davis; military figures Robert E. Lee, Ulysses S. Grant, David Farragut, and Braxton Bragg; and nurse Clara Barton, spy Rose O'Neal Greenhow, and photographer Mathew Brady. The volumes are filled with photographs, individual "Words to Know" sections, and an index.

- A cumulative index of all three titles in the American Civil War Reference Library is also available.

Acknowledgments

The authors extend thanks to Larry Baker and Tom Romig at U•X•L for their assistance throughout the production of this series. Thanks, too, to Christine Alexanian for her quick and thorough copyediting and Amy Marcaccio Keyzer for lending her considerable editorial talents in the form of proofreading. The editor wishes to thank Marco Di Vita at Graphix Group for always working with common sense, flexibility, speed, and, above all, quality. Admiration, love, and a warm hug go to Beth Baker for her year of bravery. And, finally, a very special hello goes to Charlie and Dane, whose decision to move up their pub date made the Summer of '99 so very interesting.

Comments and suggestions

We welcome your comments on *American Civil War: Primary Sources* and suggestions for other topics in history to consider. Please write: Editors, *American Civil War: Primary Sources,* U•X•L, 27500 Drake Rd., Farmington Hills, Michigan 48331-3535; call toll-free: 800-877-4253; fax to 248-414-5043; or send e-mail via http://www.galegroup.com.

American Civil War Timeline

1775   Philadelphia Quakers organize America's first antislavery society.

1776–83 English colonies' War for Independence against Great Britain ends with the formation of the United States.

1788   The U.S. Constitution is ratified, providing legal protection to slaveowners.

1793   Eli Whitney invents the cotton gin, which will dramatically increase Southern cotton production.

1803   President Thomas Jefferson purchases the Louisiana Territory from France.

1775
"Yankee Doodle" is written.

1789
George Washington takes office as the first U.S. president.

1800
The Library of Congress is established.

1775   1789   1800

1816 The American Colonization Society is formed with the idea of settling free blacks back in Africa.

1820 Congress passes the Missouri Compromise, which maintains the balance between slave and free states in the Union.

1828 Congress passes the so-called "Tariff of Abominations" over the objections of Southern states.

1831 Slave Nat Turner leads a violent slave rebellion in Virginia.

1832–33 The "Nullification Crisis" in South Carolina ends after tariffs on foreign goods are lowered.

1833 The Female Anti-Slavery Society and the American Anti-Slavery Society are founded.

1837 Abolitionist Elijah P. Lovejoy is murdered by a proslavery mob in Illinois.

1845 Texas is annexed by the United States over the objections of Mexico, which regards it as part of its country.

1848 The Mexican War ends with the United States acquiring five hundred thousand square miles of additional land in western North America.

1850 The Compromise of 1850, including the controversial Fugitive Slave Act, becomes law.

1852 Harriet Beecher Stowe's novel *Uncle Tom's Cabin* is published, increasing support for the abolitionist movement in the North.

1854 The Kansas-Nebraska Act is passed, returning decisions about allowing slavery back to individual states.

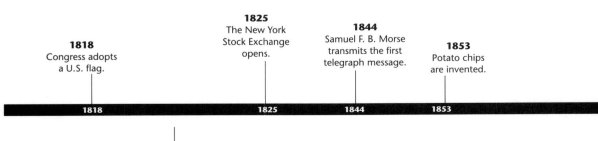

1818
Congress adopts
a U.S. flag.

1825
The New York
Stock Exchange
opens.

1844
Samuel F. B. Morse
transmits the first
telegraph message.

1853
Potato chips
are invented.

| 1818 | 1825 | 1844 | 1853 |

1857 The U.S. Supreme Court issues its famous *Dred Scott* decision, which increases Northern fears about the spread of slavery.

1858 Illinois senate candidates Abraham Lincoln and Stephen Douglas meet in their famous debates over slavery and its future place in America.

1859 Abolitionist John Brown leads a raid on Harpers Ferry, Virginia, in an unsuccessful effort to start a slave revolt across the South.

5/18/1860 The Republican Party nominates Abraham Lincoln as its candidate for president.

11/6/1860 Abraham Lincoln is elected president of the United States.

12/20/1860 South Carolina secedes from the Union.

1/9/1861 Mississippi secedes from the Union.

1/10/1861 Florida secedes from the Union.

1/11/1861 Alabama secedes from the Union.

1/19/1861 Georgia secedes from the Union.

1/26/1861 Louisiana secedes from the Union.

1/29/1861 Kansas is admitted into the Union as the thirty-fourth state.

2/1/1861 Texas secedes from the Union.

2/8/1861 The Confederate Constitution is adopted in Montgomery, Alabama.

2/9/1861 Jefferson Davis is elected provisional president of the Confederacy.

2/18/1861 Jefferson Davis is inaugurated as the president of the Confederacy.

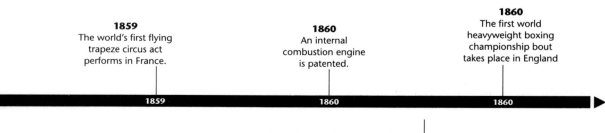

1859
The world's first flying trapeze circus act performs in France.

1860
An internal combustion engine is patented.

1860
The first world heavyweight boxing championship bout takes place in England

1859   1860   1860

3/4/1861 Abraham Lincoln is inaugurated as the sixteenth president of the United States.

3/6/1861 The Confederacy calls for one hundred thousand volunteers to join its military.

4/12/1861 South Carolina troops open fire on Fort Sumter, marking the beginning of the American Civil War.

4/13/1861 Major Robert Anderson surrenders Fort Sumter to the Confederates.

4/15/1861 President Abraham Lincoln calls for seventy-five thousand volunteers to join the Union army.

4/19/1861 President Abraham Lincoln orders a blockade of Southern ports.

5/6/1861 Arkansas secedes from the Union.

5/7/1861 Tennessee forms an alliance with the Confederacy that makes it a Confederate state for all practical purposes.

5/13/1861 Queen Victoria proclaims British neutrality in the conflict between America's Northern and Southern sections.

5/20/1861 North Carolina secedes from the Union.

5/23/1861 Virginia secedes from the Union.

6/3/1861 Stephen A. Douglas dies in Chicago, Illinois.

6/10/1861 Napoleon III declares French neutrality in the American Civil War.

6/11/1861 Counties in western Virginia resist Virginia's vote to secede and set up their own government, which is loyal to the Union.

7/20/1861 Confederate Congress convenes at the Confederate capital of Richmond, Virginia.

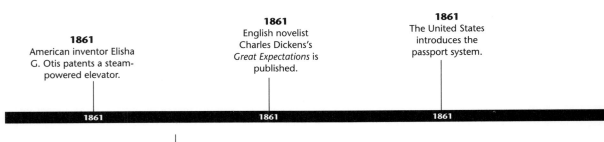

1861
American inventor Elisha G. Otis patents a steam-powered elevator.

1861
English novelist Charles Dickens's *Great Expectations* is published.

1861
The United States introduces the passport system.

1861　　　　1861　　　　1861

7/21/1861 Confederate forces win the First Battle of Bull Run, the war's first major battle.

7/25/1861 U.S. Congress passes the Crittenden Resolution, which states that the North's war aim is to preserve the Union, not end slavery.

7/27/1861 General George McClellan assumes command of Federal forces in Washington.

8/30/1861 Union general John Frémont proclaims martial law in Missouri, which is torn by violence between pro-Union and pro-Confederate forces.

11/6/1861 Jefferson Davis is elected to a six-year term as president of the Confederacy.

11/8/1861 Union Captain Charles Wilkes seizes two Confederate officials traveling on the *Trent,* a British vessel. The incident triggers deep outrage in England.

11/20/1861 The Union organizes the Joint Committee on the Conduct of the War in order to review the actions and qualifications of the North's military leadership.

11/27/1861 Confederate officials seized from the *Trent* are released from custody with apologies.

2/6/1862 Union general Ulysses S. Grant captures Fort Henry on the Tennessee River.

2/16/1862 Ulysses S. Grant captures Fort Donelson on the Cumberland River.

2/22/1862 Jefferson Davis is inaugurated as president of the Confederacy.

2/25/1862 Confederates abandon Nashville, Tennessee, to oncoming Union forces.

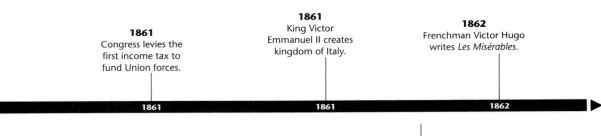

1861
Congress levies the first income tax to fund Union forces.

1861
King Victor Emmanuel II creates kingdom of Italy.

1862
Frenchman Victor Hugo writes *Les Misérables.*

1861   1861   1862

3/9/1862 The Union ship *Monitor* battles the Confederate ship *Virginia* to a draw at Hampton Roads, Virginia.

4/6–7/1862 Union and Confederate forces battle in the inconclusive Battle of Shiloh in Tennessee.

4/16/1862 The Confederate Congress passes a conscription act requiring most able-bodied men between the ages of eighteen and thirty-five to sign up for military service.

4/25/1862 The Union fleet under the command of Admiral David Farragut captures New Orleans.

6/1/1862 General Robert E. Lee assumes command of Confederate forces defending Richmond, Virginia.

6/6/1862 Union forces take control of Memphis, Tennessee.

6/17/1862 Confederate forces led by Stonewall Jackson leave the Shenandoah Valley after a successful military campaign.

6/25/1862 The Seven Days' Battles begin between George McClellan's Army of the Potomac and Robert E. Lee's Army of Northern Virginia.

7/2/1862 President Abraham Lincoln calls for three hundred thousand enlistments for three-year periods in order to further strengthen the Union army.

7/17/1862 U.S. Congress passes laws allowing blacks to serve as soldiers in Union army.

7/29/1862 Confederate commerce raider *Alabama* leaves England and starts attacking Northern trading vessels.

8/29–30/1862 The Second Battle of Bull Run ends in a disastrous defeat for the Union.

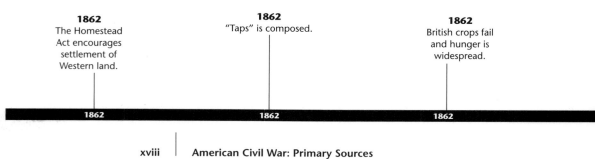

1862
The Homestead Act encourages settlement of Western land.

1862
"Taps" is composed.

1862
British crops fail and hunger is widespread.

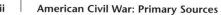

1862   1862   1862

American Civil War: Primary Sources

9/5/1862 General Robert E. Lee leads the Army of Northern Virginia into Northern territory for the first time, as his force enters Maryland.

9/15/1862 Stonewall Jackson's army captures twelve thousand Union troops at Harpers Ferry, Virginia.

9/17/1862 George McClellan's Army of the Potomac and Robert E. Lee's Army of Northern Virginia fight at Antietam in the bloodiest single day of the war. Neither side registers a conclusive victory, but the draw convinces Lee to return to Virginia.

9/22/1862 President Abraham Lincoln issues his preliminary Emancipation Proclamation, which will free slaves in Confederate territory.

10/8/1862 Confederate invasion of Kentucky ends after the Battle of Perryville.

10/12/1862 Jeb Stuart's Confederate cavalry completes ride around George McClellan's Union army after raid on Chambersburg, Pennsylvania.

11/7/1862 President Abraham Lincoln removes General George McClellan from command of the Army of the Potomac, replacing him with General Ambrose Burnside.

12/13/1862 General Robert E. Lee's Confederate forces hand the Union a decisive defeat at the Battle of Fredericksburg.

1/1/1863 President Abraham Lincoln issues the Emancipation Proclamation, which frees all slaves in Confederate territory.

1/2/1863 Union victory at the Battle of Stones River stops Confederate plans to invade middle Tennessee.

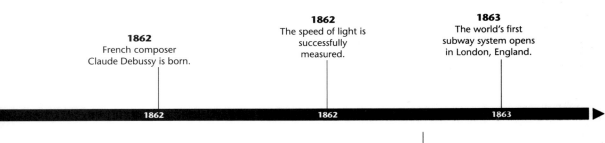

1862
French composer Claude Debussy is born.

1862
The speed of light is successfully measured.

1863
The world's first subway system opens in London, England.

1862   1862   1863

American Civil War Timeline   xix

1/23/1863 General Ambrose Burnside's new offensive against Robert E. Lee's Army of Northern Virginia sputters to a halt in bad weather. Burnside's "Mud March" convinces President Abraham Lincoln to replace him with General Joseph Hooker.

3/3/1863 U.S. Congress passes a conscription act requiring most able-bodied Northern men to sign up for military service.

4/2/1863 Bread riots erupt in Richmond, Virginia, as hungry civilians resort to violence to feed their families.

5/2/1863 General Robert E. Lee and the Confederates claim a big victory at Chancellorsville, but Stonewall Jackson is killed during the battle.

5/22/1863 General Ulysses S. Grant begins the siege of Vicksburg, Mississippi, after attempts to take the Confederate stronghold by force are turned back.

6/9/1863 The largest cavalry battle of the Civil War ends in a draw at Brandy Station, Virginia.

6/20/1863 West Virginia is admitted into the Union as the thirty-fifth state.

7/1–3/1863 The famous Battle of Gettysburg takes place in Pennsylvania. Union general George Meade and the Army of the Potomac successfully turn back General Robert E. Lee's attempted invasion of the North, doing terrible damage to Lee's Army of Northern Virginia in the process.

7/4/1863 Vicksburg surrenders to General Ulysses S. Grant and his Union force after a six-week siege of the city.

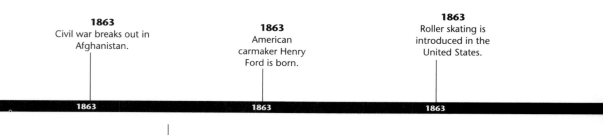

1863
Civil war breaks out in Afghanistan.

1863
American carmaker Henry Ford is born.

1863
Roller skating is introduced in the United States.

1863   1863   1863

7/9/1863 Union troops take control of Port Hudson, Louisiana. The victory gives the North control of the Mississippi River.

7/13/1863 Antidraft mobs begin four days of rioting in New York City.

7/18/1863 Black troops of the Fifty-Fourth Massachusetts regiment make a valiant but unsuccessful attempt to seize Fort Wagner in South Carolina from the Confederates.

8/21/1863 Confederate raiders led by William C. Quantrill murder 150 antislavery settlers and burn large sections of Lawrence, Kansas.

9/2/1863 Union troops take control of Knoxville, Tennessee.

9/9/1863 Union forces take control of Chattanooga, Tennessee, after the city is abandoned by General Braxton Bragg's army.

9/20/1863 The two-day Battle of Chickamauga ends in a major defeat for the Union.

9/23/1863 General Braxton Bragg begins the Confederate siege of Chattanooga.

10/17/1863 General Ulysses S. Grant is named supreme commander of Union forces in the west.

11/19/1863 President Abraham Lincoln delivers his famous Gettysburg Address at a ceremony dedicating a cemetery for soldiers who died at the Battle of Gettysburg in Pennsylvania.

11/25/1863 The three-day Battle of Chattanooga results in a major victory for the North, as Union troops led by General George Henry Thomas scatter General Braxton Bragg's Confederate army.

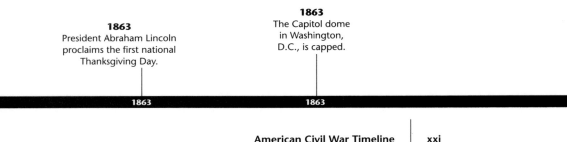

1863
President Abraham Lincoln proclaims the first national Thanksgiving Day.

1863
The Capitol dome in Washington, D.C., is capped.

1863   1863

12/8/1863 President Abraham Lincoln proposes his Ten Percent Plan, which says that seceded states can return to the Union provided that one-tenth of the 1860 voters agree to form a state government that is loyal to the Union.

12/27/1863 General Joseph Johnston takes command of the Confederate Army of Tennessee.

3/12/1864 General Ulysses S. Grant is promoted to leadership of all of the Union armies.

3/18/1864 General William T. Sherman is named to lead Union armies in the west.

4/12/1864 Confederate troops led by Nathan Bedford Forrest capture Fort Pillow, Tennessee, and are accused of murdering black Union soldiers stationed there.

4/17/1864 General Ulysses S. Grant calls a halt to prisoner exchanges between North and South, further increasing the Confederacy's manpower problems.

5/5/1864 General Robert E. Lee's Army of Northern Virginia and General Ulysses S. Grant's Army of the Potomac battle in the Wilderness campaign.

5/9–12/1864 General Robert E. Lee stops the Union advance on Richmond at the brutal Battle of Spotsylvania.

5/11/1864 Jeb Stuart is mortally wounded in a battle with Philip Sheridan's cavalry at Brandy Station, Virginia.

6/1864 U.S. Congress passes a law providing for equal pay for black and white soldiers.

6/3/1864 The Union's Army of the Potomac suffers heavy losses in a failed assault on Robert E. Lee's army at Cold Harbor, Virginia.

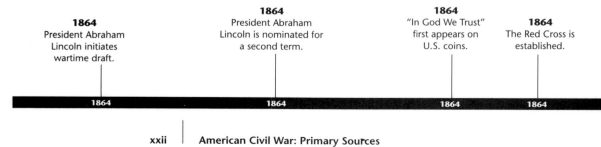

1864
President Abraham Lincoln initiates wartime draft.

1864
President Abraham Lincoln is nominated for a second term.

1864
"In God We Trust" first appears on U.S. coins.

1864
The Red Cross is established.

1864　　　　　　1864　　　　　　1864　　1864

6/18/1864 General Ulysses S. Grant begins the Union siege of Petersburg, which is defended by Robert E. Lee's Army of Northern Virginia.

6/23/1864 Confederate forces led by Jubal Early begin a campaign in the Shenandoah Valley.

7/11/1864 Confederate troops commanded by Jubal Early reach outskirts of Washington, D.C., before being forced to return to the Shenandoah Valley.

7/17/1864 General John Bell Hood takes command of the Confederate Army of Tennessee.

8/5/1864 Admiral David Farragut leads the Union Navy to a major victory in the Battle of Mobile Bay, which closes off one of the Confederacy's last remaining ports.

8/29/1864 The Democratic Party nominates General George McClellan as its candidate for president of the United States and pushes a campaign promising an end to the war.

9/1/1864 General William T. Sherman captures Atlanta, Georgia, after a long campaign.

9/4/1864 General William T. Sherman orders all civilians to leave Atlanta, Georgia, as a way to hurt Southern morale.

9/19–22/1864 Union troops led by Philip Sheridan defeat Jubal Early's Confederate army in the Shenandoah Valley.

10/6/1864 Philip Sheridan's Union troops begin a campaign of destruction in the Shenandoah Valley in order to wipe out Confederate sympathizers and sources of supplies.

10/19/1864 Philip Sheridan's army drives Jubal Early's Confederate force out of the Shenandoah Valley.

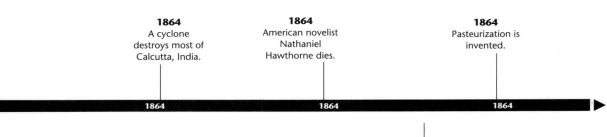

1864
A cyclone destroys most of Calcutta, India.

1864
American novelist Nathaniel Hawthorne dies.

1864
Pasteurization is invented.

1864

1864

1864

10/31/1864 Nevada is admitted into the Union as the thirty-sixth state.

11/8/1864 Abraham Lincoln is reelected to the presidency of the United States by a comfortable margin.

11/15/1864 General William T. Sherman begins his famous March to the Sea, in which his Union army destroys a large area of Georgia on its way to the port city of Savannah.

12/16/1864 Union forces under the command of General George Henry Thomas crush John Bell Hood's Army of Tennessee at the Battle of Nashville.

12/21/1864 William T. Sherman's Union army completes its March to the Sea by taking control of Savannah, Georgia.

1/31/1865 The U.S. Congress submits the Thirteenth Amendment, which abolishes slavery, to the individual states for passage.

2/17/1865 General William T. Sherman's army occupies the South Carolina capital of Columbia.

2/18/1865 Union forces seize control of Charleston, South Carolina.

2/22/1865 Confederate president Jefferson Davis returns command of the Army of Tennessee to General Joseph Johnston in a desperate attempt to stop William T. Sherman's advance into North Carolina.

3/2/1865 Remaining Confederate troops in Shenandoah Valley go down to defeat at the hands of Philip Sheridan.

3/4/1865 President Abraham Lincoln is inaugurated for a second term of office.

3/13/1865 The Confederate Congress authorizes the use of slaves as Confederate combat soldiers.

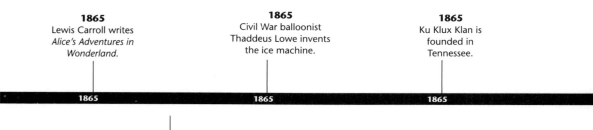

1865
Lewis Carroll writes
*Alice's Adventures in
Wonderland.*

1865
Civil War balloonist
Thaddeus Lowe invents
the ice machine.

1865
Ku Klux Klan is
founded in
Tennessee.

1865   1865   1865

4/1–2/1865 Ulysses S. Grant's Army of the Potomac successfully breaks through Confederate defenses at Petersburg, forcing Robert E. Lee's Army of Northern Virginia to evacuate the city and give up its defense of Richmond, Virginia.

4/3/1865 Union troops take control of Richmond, Virginia, and prepare for a visit from President Abraham Lincoln a day later.

4/9/1865 Trapped by pursuing Federal troops, General Robert E. Lee surrenders to General Ulysses S. Grant at Appomattox in Virginia.

4/14/1865 President Abraham Lincoln is shot by John Wilkes Booth while attending a play at Ford's Theatre in Washington, D.C.

4/15/1865 Vice president Andrew Johnson becomes president after Abraham Lincoln dies.

4/18/1865 Confederate General Joseph Johnston surrenders his Army of Tennessee to William T. Sherman near Raleigh, North Carolina.

4/26/1865 John Wilkes Booth is killed by Federal soldiers in a barn near Bowling Green, Virginia.

5/10/1865 Confederate president Jefferson Davis is taken prisoner by Federal troops at Irwinsville, Georgia.

5/26/1865 The very last Confederate troops put down their weapons, as a rebel army west of the Mississippi River led by Kirby Smith surrenders to Union officials.

6/6/1865 William Quantrill dies in federal prison.

1866 The Republican Congress passes a Civil Rights Act over President Andrew Johnson's veto. The Act gives citizenship and other rights to black people.

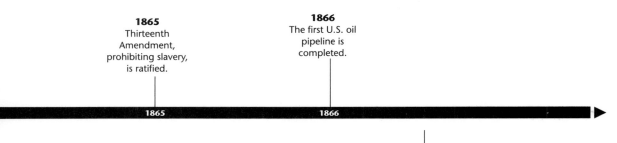

1865
Thirteenth Amendment, prohibiting slavery, is ratified.

1866
The first U.S. oil pipeline is completed.

1865

1866

1866	Race riots between blacks and whites erupt during the summer in Memphis, Tennessee, and New Orleans, Louisiana.
1866	Tennessee is readmitted into the Union by Congress.
1866	George M. Maddox of Quantrill's Raiders is acquitted of murder charges from massacre at Lawrence, Kansas.
1867	Congress passes the Military Reconstruction Act over President Andrew Johnson's veto.
1867	The Ku Klux Klan adopts a formal constitution and selects former Confederate general Nathan Bedford Forrest as its first leader.
1867	Former Confederate president Jefferson Davis is released from a Virginia jail after two years of imprisonment.
1868	Political disagreements between Congress and President Andrew Johnson become so great that the president is impeached. He avoids being removed from office by one vote in his Senate impeachment trial.
1868	Congress passes the Fifteenth Amendment, which extends voting rights to blacks, and sends the bill along to individual states for ratification.
1868	Alabama, Arkansas, Florida, Louisiana, North Carolina, and South Carolina are readmitted into the Union by Congress.
1868	Republican Ulysses S. Grant is elected the eighteenth president of the United States.
1868	Georgia expels black representatives, saying they are not eligible to hold political office. U.S. Congress responds by refusing to recognize Georgia representatives.

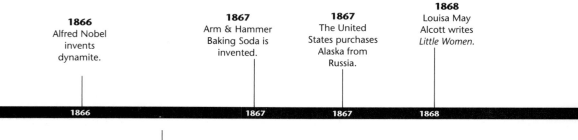

1866
Alfred Nobel
invents
dynamite.

1867
Arm & Hammer
Baking Soda is
invented.

1867
The United
States purchases
Alaska from
Russia.

1868
Louisa May
Alcott writes
Little Women.

1866   1867   1867   1868

1868   Federal government sends troops back into Georgia to reestablish military law.

1870   The Fifteenth Amendment, guaranteeing voting rights for blacks, is ratified by the states and becomes law.

1870   Congress passes the Enforcement Act of 1870 in an effort to protect the voting rights of all citizens—especially blacks—in the South.

1870   Georgia, Mississippi, Virginia, and Texas are readmitted into the Union by Congress.

1871   Congress passes the Ku Klux Klan Act, which outlaws conspiracies, use of disguises, and other practices of the white supremacist group.

1872   Ulysses S. Grant is reelected president of the United States.

1875   Congress passes a Civil Rights Act barring discrimination in hotels, theaters, railroads, and other public places.

1876   Republican Rutherford B. Hayes and Democrat Samuel J. Tilden run a very close race for the presidency of the United States. Tilden wins the popular vote, but neither candidate receives enough electoral votes for election. The two political parties eventually agree to a compromise in which Hayes becomes president in exchange for a guarantee that he remove federal troops from South Carolina, Florida, and Louisiana.

1877   President Rutherford B. Hayes removes Federal troops from the South. This withdrawal increases the vulnerability of blacks to Southern racism and marks the end of the Reconstruction period in American history.

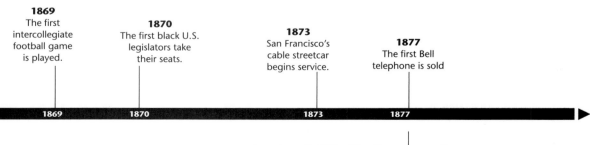

1869
The first intercollegiate football game is played.

1870
The first black U.S. legislators take their seats.

1873
San Francisco's cable streetcar begins service.

1877
The first Bell telephone is sold

1869   1870   1873   1877

A map of the United States east of the Mississippi River shows the key battles and events of the Civil War. *(Illustration by XNR Productions. Reproduced by permission of The Gale Group.)*

Research and Activity Ideas

The following research and activity ideas are intended to offer suggestions for complementing social studies and history curricula, to trigger additional ideas for enhancing learning, and to suggest cross-disciplinary projects for library and classroom use.

Divide into two groups. One group will discuss the arguments of people who felt that elimination of slavery should be the Union's most important war aim. The other group will consider the various reasons that other people felt that restoration of the Union was the most important goal. Then have a representative from one group assume the identity of black abolitionist Frederick Douglass, while a member of the other group plays the role of President Abraham Lincoln. Pretend that Douglass has been granted a meeting with the president. Have Douglass try to convince Lincoln to make the destruction of slavery his primary war aim. Have the president defend the idea of making preservation of the Union his primary goal.

After Harriet Beecher Stowe's *Uncle Tom's Cabin* was published, people reacted to the book in many different ways. Have students write a one-page written response to the book from the perspective of one of the following four people: a Southern plantation owner who has lost several slaves to the Underground Railroad; a Northern abolitionist; a former slave who has secured freedom in the North; and a Southern white woman with children of her own.

Pretend that you are a former slave who is now free because the Union army has taken control of the region in which you live. Some other former slaves have decided to join the Union military. Should you join, too? Divide the class into two groups. Have one group pretend that it is making this decision in October 1862, before black soldiers were paid at the same rate as white soldiers. Have the other group pretend that it is making this decision in July 1864, after the Union agreed to give black and white soldiers the same pay. Each student will compose a two-column list in which he or she lists the positive and negative factors associated with joining the Union army. Then each student will write a page explaining his or her final decision about whether or not to enlist.

Research various responses to General William T. Sherman's capture and destruction of Atlanta in 1864 in both the North and South. Then write two different newspaper articles on Sherman's actions. In the first, pretend that you are writing for a Northern newspaper such as the *New York Times*. In the second article, pretend that you are writing for a Southern paper like the *Richmond Whig*.

Review the reactions in both the North and the South to news of Robert E. Lee's surrender and Abraham Lincoln's assassination. Then divide the class into four groups. Each group will play the parts of Civil War soldiers during the final days of the war. Two of the groups will play the roles of Union soldiers, while the other two groups will play the parts of Confederate soldiers. Assign one Union group and one Confederate group to react to news of Lee's surrender. The other two groups will react to news of the Lincoln assassination.

Pretend that you are a Union or Confederate soldier writing a letter home before going into battle for the first time. Discuss the reasons why you enlisted in the army, and your emotions as you prepare to face enemy gunfire.

Study the Southern reaction to Stonewall Jackson's death, and prepare a written or oral report explaining why his death had such an impact throughout the Confederacy.

Research the wartime activities of Confederate guerrillas and conditions across the South in 1865. Then write a report explaining why most historians agree that Robert E. Lee's decision to surrender rather than approve guerrilla activity was a good one.

Imagine that you are a slave on a plantation in the South in 1863. Write a one-page paper describing how you would react upon hearing about the Emancipation Proclamation for the first time. How would you feel? What would you do next? Would it make any difference if you had a family? Now imagine that you are a Union soldier who has just heard about the Emancipation Proclamation. Write a few paragraphs describing your reaction. Would it affect the way you think about the war?

Pretend that you are a young man living in either the North or the South in 1861. Upon learning about the Confederate attack on Fort Sumter, you decide to enlist in your side's army. Write a letter to a friend or relative living in the other half of the country explaining your decision. Keep in mind that you may end up facing them on the battlefield.

There were three main branches of military service during the Civil War: artillery, infantry, and cavalry. Research what daily life was like for members of each branch of service. If you were a soldier, which branch would you have wanted to serve in? Write a one-page paper explaining your decision. Would your decision change depending on whether you were a Union or Confederate soldier?

Harriet Beecher Stowe

Excerpt from Uncle Tom's Cabin
First published in 1852

A novel about the evils of slavery

In the years leading up to the Civil War, growing numbers of people wanted to abolish (put an end to) slavery in the United States. People who actively fought to end slavery were known as abolitionists. During the 1830s and 1840s, abolitionists distributed millions of antislavery newsletters and pamphlets in Northern cities. The abolitionist movement gradually gained strength and became more vocal during this time. But slavery remained important to the cotton-growing economy of the South. In addition, many people continued to believe that black people were inferior to white people and did not deserve the same rights. As a result, most Southerners were determined to resist the abolitionists' efforts to interfere with their way of life.

> "'Lucy,' said the trader, 'your child's gone; you may as well know it first as last. You see, I know'd you couldn't take him down south; and I got a chance to sell him to a first-rate family, that'll raise him better than you can.'"
>
> *From* Uncle Tom's Cabin

In 1850, Southerners in the U.S. Congress passed the Fugitive Slave Act. This measure granted slaveowners sweeping new powers to capture and reclaim escaped slaves. It also required people in the North to assist the slaveowners in retrieving their property. Many Northerners resented the Fugitive Slave Act. They were able to ignore slavery when it was confined to the South, but not when they saw black people being tracked down like animals and carried off in chains within their own cities. Some people simply disobeyed the act. Others became active in helping escaped slaves hide or reach Canada, where slavery was not allowed. The Fugitive Slave Act ended up increasing the antislavery and anti-Southern feelings of many people in the North.

The Fugitive Slave Act had a strong effect on a young writer named Harriet Beecher Stowe (1811–1896). The daughter of prominent religious leader Lyman Beecher (1775–1863), Stowe was born in Litchfield, Connecticut. In 1832, she moved with her family to Cincinnati, a city in the southern part of Ohio just across the Ohio River from the slave-holding state of Kentucky. Stowe occasionally encountered fugitive slaves while living in Cincinnati. She also read *American Slavery as It Is* by abolitionist Theodore Dwight Weld (1803–1895), a collection of articles about slavery and advertisements for slaves from Southern newspapers. Stowe moved to Brunswick, Maine, the same year that the Fugitive Slave Act was passed. The new law inspired her to begin a novel that became the single most important piece of antislavery literature in American history.

Stowe's work, *Uncle Tom's Cabin,* first appeared as a series of short articles in *National Era* magazine in 1851. It proved to be extremely popular with Northern readers and was published in book form in 1852. *Uncle Tom's Cabin* follows the lives of several black slaves who work for a cruel man named Simon Legree in the South. Through the experiences of Uncle Tom, Eliza, Eva, and others, the novel painted a powerful picture of the evils of slavery. It also gave readers a more realistic understanding of slaves. It was one of the first books to portray black characters as human beings with the same desires, dreams, and weaknesses as white people. *Uncle Tom's Cabin* turned out to be a perfect expression of people's guilt, anger, and disgust at seeing slaves being hunted down in the North under the Fugitive Slave Act.

One of the most powerful themes of Stowe's book involves the forced separation of black families under slavery. "Striking to the very heart of the slave's nightmare—and of the white South's guilt—she centered her novel on the helpless instability of the Negro's home life," Kenneth S. Lynn wrote in his introduction to the novel. In one sense, slaves in

America were encouraged to form families. The U.S. government had agreed to stop importing new slaves from Africa in 1808. So in order to have a continued source of labor after that time, the South needed existing slaves to reproduce.

But black family life was very fragile. Southern states did not consider the marriages of slaves to be legally binding. Husbands, wives, parents, and children could be sold separately at any time. "Even a master who himself refused to sell family members apart from each other could not always prevent such sales to settle debts after his death," James M. McPherson wrote in *Ordeal by Fire: The Civil War and Reconstruction.* "Several studies of slavery have found that from one-fifth to one-third of slave marriages were broken by owners—generally by selling one or both of the partners separately. The percentage of children sold apart from their parents or siblings cannot even be estimated."

A typical slave family of the early 1860s in front of their cabin. *(Photograph by T.H. O'Sullivan. Courtesy of the Library of Congress.)*

The following excerpt from *Uncle Tom's Cabin* comes from a chapter called "A Select Incident of Lawful Trade." It deals with the tragic practice of breaking up black families. Haley is a slave trader—a person who makes a living by traveling around and buying slaves to fill the needs of plantations in the South. Haley has already purchased Tom—the main character of *Uncle Tom's Cabin*—from the Shelby family. The Shelbys had treated their few slaves kindly and had promised not to sell them, but were forced to do so in order to pay off large debts.

Haley takes Tom with him on a boat down the Ohio River, which runs along the northern border of Kentucky and eventually meets the Mississippi River. Along the way, Haley stops at several auctions and buys other slaves. One of these slaves is a young woman named Lucy, who comes aboard with her baby. Lucy's master had told her that she was going

A depiction of a slave auction in the early 1860s. *(Reproduced by permission of Archive Photos, Inc.)*

to Louisville, Kentucky, to be a cook at a tavern where her husband worked. But once Lucy is on the boat, Haley informs her that he has bought her and plans to take her to a plantation in the South. Lucy is shocked at first, but soon realizes that she has no choice but to go along with Haley. Before long, however, something even more terrible happens. It turns out to be more than she can stand.

Things to remember while reading the excerpt from Harriet Beecher Stowe's *Uncle Tom's Cabin:*

- Stowe uses a literary device called irony in her novel—she says the opposite of what she means in order to make a point. A good example of Stowe's use of irony occurs in the following excerpt, when she describes the different reactions of Haley and Tom when Lucy's child is taken from her. When Stowe describes Haley's reaction, she says that "the trader had arrived at that stage of Christian and political perfection . . . in which he had completely overcome every humane weakness and prejudice." Haley feels no sympathy for the young mother—he has lost the basic human tendency to care about someone else. But Stowe makes it seem as if Haley's feelings are normal and right, even perfect, in the eyes of society. On the other hand, when describing the reaction of Tom, she says that the separation of mother and child "looked like something unutterably horrible and cruel, because, poor, ignorant black soul! He had not learned to generalize, and to take enlarged views." Tom feels tremendous sympathy for Lucy. But Stowe makes it seem as if Tom only feels this way because he is ignorant and cannot see the importance of slavery in Southern society. Of course, Stowe was an abolitionist who was trying to convince others that slavery was wrong. She described the two men's reactions in the opposite way that she truly felt about them in order to make a point with readers.

- After Lucy commits suicide by jumping overboard from the boat, Stowe says that she "escaped into a state which *never will* give up a fugitive,—not even at the demand of the whole glorious Union." This is a reference to the Fugitive Slave Act. Stowe is saying that, under the law, death is the only escape from slavery for some people.

- Toward the end of the excerpt, Stowe relates a conversation between two unnamed people about Haley, the slave trader. The speakers consider him—and all other slave traders—"unfeeling," "dreadful," and "universally despised." But Stowe makes it clear in the next few paragraphs that Haley is just a product of a society that allows slavery. She claims that the wealthy, educated members of society are actually worse than him, because they promote his ugly business even though they should know better.

Excerpt from Harriet Beecher Stowe's Uncle Tom's Cabin

[Lucy] *looked calm, as the boat went on; and a beautiful soft summer breeze passed like a compassionate spirit over her head,—the gentle breeze, that never inquires whether the brow is **dusky** or **fair** that it fans. And she saw sunshine sparkling on the water, in golden ripples, and heard **gay** voices, full of ease and pleasure talking around her everywhere; but her heart lay as if a great stone had fallen on it. Her baby raised himself up against her, and stroked her cheeks with his little hands; and, springing up and down, crowing and chatting, seemed determined to arouse her. She strained him suddenly and tightly in her arms, and slowly one tear after another fell on his wondering, unconscious face; and gradually she seemed, and little by little, to grow calmer, and busied herself with tending and nursing him.*

The child, a boy of ten months, was uncommonly large and strong of his age, and very vigorous in his limbs. Never, for a moment, still, he kept his mother constantly busy in holding him, and guarding his springing activity.

"Tha's a fine chap!" said a man, suddenly stopping opposite to him, with his hands in his pockets. "How old is he?"

"Ten months and a half," said the mother.

The man whistled to the boy, and offered him part of a stick of candy, which he eagerly grabbed at, and very soon had it in a baby's general depository, to wit, his mouth.

"Rum fellow!" said the man. "Know's what's what!" and he whistled, and walked on. When he had got to the other side of the boat, he came across Haley, who was smoking on top of a pile of boxes.

*The stranger produced a match, lighted a cigar, saying, as he did so, "**Decentish** kind o' **wench** you've got round there, stranger."*

*"Why, I **reckon** she is **tol'able** fair," said Haley, blowing the smoke out of his mouth.*

"Taking her down south?" said the man.

Dusky: Dark.

Fair: Light in color.

Gay: Happy.

Decentish: Somewhat decent.

Wench: A young woman or female servant.

Reckon: Think or suppose.

Tol'able: Tolerable; acceptable.

Haley nodded, and smoked on.

"Plantation hand?" said the man.

"Wal," said Haley, "I'm fillin' out an order for a plantation, and I think I shall put her in. They told me she was a good cook; and they can use her for that, or set her at the cotton-picking. She's got the right fingers for that, I looked at 'em. Sell well, either way;" and Haley resumed his cigar.

"They won't want the young 'un on the plantation," said the man.

"I shall sell him, first chance I find," said Haley, lighting another cigar.

"S'pose you'd be selling him tol'able cheap," said the stranger, mounting the pile of boxes, and sitting down comfortably.

"Don't know 'bout that," said Haley; "he's a pretty smart young 'un,—straight, fat, strong; flesh as hard as a brick!"

"Very true, but then there's the bother and expense of raisin'."

"Nonsense!" said Haley; "they is raised as easy as any kind of critter there is going; they an't a bit more trouble than pups. This **yer** chap will be running all around, in a month."

"I've got a good place for raisin', and I thought of takin' in a little more **stock**," said the man. "One cook lost a young 'un last week,—got drownded in a wash-tub, while she was a hangin' out clothes,—and I reckon it would be well enough to set her to raisin' this yer."

Haley and the stranger smoked a while in silence. . . . [The two men argue back and forth, and finally settle on a price of $45 for the baby.]

"Done!" said Haley. "Where do you land?"

"At Louisville," said the man.

"Louisville," said Haley. "Very fair, we get there about dusk. Chap will be asleep,—all fair,—get him off quietly, and no screaming,—happens beautiful,—I like to do everything quietly,—I hates all kind of **agitation** and fluster." And so, after a transfer of certain bills had passed from the man's pocket-book to the trader's, he resumed his cigar.

It was a bright, tranquil evening when the boat stopped at the **wharf** at Louisville. The woman had been sitting with her baby in

Yer: Here.

Stock: Short for live stock, meaning slaves.

Agitation: Trouble or disturbance.

Wharf: A structure built along the bank of a river that allows ships to load and unload passengers and cargo.

her arms, now wrapped in a heavy sleep. When she heard the name of the place called out, she hastily laid the child down in a little cradle formed by the hollow among the boxes, first carefully spreading under it her **cloak**; and then she sprung to the side of the boat, in hopes that, among the various hotel-waiters who **thronged** the wharf, she might see her husband. In this hope, she pressed forward to the front rails, and, stretching far over them, strained her eyes intently on the moving heads on the shore, and the crowd pressed in between her and the child.

"Now's your time," said Haley, taking the sleeping child up, and handing him to the stranger. "Don't wake him up, and set him to crying, now; it would make a devil of a fuss with the gal." The man took the bundle carefully, and was soon lost in the crowd that went up the wharf.

When the boat, creaking, and groaning, and puffing, had loosed from the wharf, and was beginning slowly to strain herself along, the woman returned to her old seat. The trader was sitting there,—the child was gone!

"Why, why,—where?" she began, in **bewildered** surprise.

"Lucy," said the trader, "your child's gone; you may as well know it first as last. You see, I know'd you couldn't take him down south; and I got a chance to sell him to a first-rate family, that'll raise him better than you can."

The trader had arrived at that stage of Christian and political perfection which has been recommended by some preachers and politicians of the north, lately, in which he had completely overcome every human weakness and prejudice. His heart was exactly where yours, sir, and mine could be brought, with proper effort and **cultivation**. The wild look of **anguish** and utter despair that the woman cast on him might have disturbed one less practised; but he was used to it. He had seen that same look hundreds of times. You can get used to such things, too, my friend; and it is the great object of recent efforts to make our whole northern community used to them, for the glory of the Union. So the trader only regarded the mortal anguish which he saw working in those dark features, those clenched hands, and suffocating breathings, as necessary incidents of the trade, and merely calculated whether she was going to scream, and get up a **commotion** on the boat; for like other supporters of our **peculiar institution**, he decidedly disliked agitation.

Cloak: A loose-fitting outer garment, like a coat or cape.

Thronged: Pressed forward or crowded in upon.

Bewildered: Puzzled or confused.

Cultivation: Growth or improvement that comes from work or study.

Anguish: Extreme pain, distress, or sorrow.

Commotion: Disturbance.

Peculiar institution: A term for slavery.

But the woman did not scream. The shot had passed too straight and direct through the heart, for cry or tear.

Dizzily she sat down. Her **slack** hands fell lifeless by her side. Her eyes looked straight forward, but she saw nothing. All the noise and hum of the boat, the groaning of the machinery, mingled dreamily to her bewildered ear; and the poor, **dumb-stricken** heart had neither cry nor tear to show for its utter misery. She was quite calm.

The trader, who, considering his advantages, was almost as humane as some of our politicians, seemed to feel called on to administer such **consolation** as the case admitted of. . . . [Haley tries to console Lucy, telling her that she will find a nice place and a new husband down river. She begs him not to talk to her.]

The trader walked up and down for a time, and occasionally stopped and looked at her.

"Takes it hard, rather," he **soliloquized,** "but quiet, tho';—let her sweat a while; she'll come right, by and by!"

Tom had watched the whole transaction from first to last, and had a perfect understanding of its results. To him, it looked like something unutterably horrible and cruel, because, poor, ignorant black soul! He had not learned to **generalize,** and to take enlarged views. If he had only been instructed by certain ministers of Christianity, he might have thought better of it, and seen in it an every-day incident of a **lawful trade;** a trade which is the vital support of an institution which an American **divine** tells us has "no evils but such as are inseparable from any other relations in social and domestic life." But Tom, as we see, being a poor, ignorant fellow, whose reading had been confined entirely to the New Testament, could not comfort and **solace** himself with views like these. His very soul bled within him for what seemed to him the wrongs of the poor suffering thing that lay like a crushed reed on the boxes; the feeling, living, bleeding, yet immortal thing, which American state law coolly classes with the bundles, and bales, and boxes, among which she is lying.

Tom drew near, and tried to say something; but she only groaned. Honestly, and with tears running down his own cheeks, he spoke of a heart of love in the skies, of a pitying Jesus, and an **eternal home;** but the ear was deaf with anguish, and the **palsied** heart could not feel.

Night came on,—night calm, unmoved, and glorious, shining down with her **innumerable** and solemn angel eyes, twinkling,

Slack: Weak.

Dumb-stricken: Made unable to speak by shock or astonishment.

Consolation: Comfort.

Soliloquized: Said to himself.

Generalize: Expand the details of a particular situation to form an overall conclusion or widely applicable principle.

Lawful trade: A legal and accepted job or occupation.

Divine: Clergyman or preacher.

Solace: Console or provide relief from grief or anxiety.

Eternal home: Heaven.

Palsied: Paralyzed.

Innumerable: Countless.

beautiful, but silent. There was no speech nor language, no pitying voice or helping hand, from that distant sky. One after another, the voices of business or pleasure died away; all on the boat were sleeping, and the ripples at the **prow** were plainly heard. Tom stretched himself out on a box, and there, as he lay, he heard, **ever and anon,** a smothered sob or cry from the **prostrate** creature,—"O! What shall I do? O Lord! O good Lord, do help me!" and so, ever and anon, until the murmur died away in silence.

At midnight, Tom waked, with a sudden start. Something black passed quickly by him to the side of the boat, and he heard a splash in the water. No one else saw or heard anything. He raised his head,—the woman's place was vacant! He got up, and sought about him in vain. The poor bleeding heart was still, at last, and the river rippled and dimpled just as brightly as if it had not closed above it.

Patience! patience! Ye whose hearts swell **indignant** at wrongs like these. Not one throb of anguish, not one tear of the oppressed, is forgotten by the Man of Sorrows, the Lord of Glory. In his patient, generous bosom he bears the anguish of a world. Bear thou, like him, in patience, and labor in love; for sure as he is God, "the year of his redeemed shall come."

The trader waked up bright and early, and came out to see to his **live stock.** It was now his turn to look about in **perplexity.** "Where alive is that gal?" he said to Tom.

Tom, who had learned the wisdom of **keeping counsel,** did not feel called upon to state his observations and suspicions, but said he did not know.

"She surely couldn't have got off in the night at any of the landings, for I was awake, and on the look-out, whenever the boat stopped. I never trust these yer things to other folks."

This speech was addressed to Tom quite confidentially, as if it was something that would be specially interesting to him. Tom made no answer.

The trader searched the boat from **stem to stern**, among boxes, bales, and barrels, around the machinery, by the chimneys, in vain.

"Now, I say, Tom, be fair about this yer," he said, when, after a fruitless search, he came where Tom was standing. "You know something about it, now. Don't tell me,—I know you do. I saw the gal stretched out here about ten o'clock, and ag'in at twelve, and

Prow: Forward part of a ship.

Ever and anon: Now and again.

Prostrate: Lying flat, lacking the will or power to rise.

Indignant: Expressing anger at an unjust act or situation.

Live stock: Slaves.

Perplexity: Confusion.

Keeping counsel: Guarding his thoughts or intentions.

Stem to stern: Front to back; thoroughly.

ag'in between one and two; and then at four she was gone, and you was a sleeping right there all the time. Now, you know something,—you can't help it."

*"Well, **Mas'r**," said Tom, "towards morning something brushed by me, and I kinder half woke; and then I hearn a great splash, and then I clare woke up, and the gal was gone. That's all I know on 't."*

*The trader was not shocked nor amazed; because, as we said before, he was used to a great many things that you are not used to. Even the awful presence of Death struck no solemn chill upon him. He had seen Death many times,—met him in the way of trade, and got acquainted with him,—and he only thought of him as a hard customer, that **embarrassed** his **property operations** very unfairly; and so he only swore that the gal was a baggage, and that he was devilishly unlucky, and that, if things went on in this way, he should not make a cent on the trip. In short, he seemed to consider himself an **ill-used man**, decidedly; but there was no help for it, as the woman had escaped into a state which* never will *give up a fugitive,—not even at the demand of the whole glorious Union. The trader, therefore, sat **discontentedly** down, with his little account-book, and put down the missing body and soul under the head of* losses!

"He's a shocking creature, isn't he,—this trader? so unfeeling! It's dreadful, really!"

"O, but nobody thinks anything of these traders! They are universally despised,—never received into any decent society."

*But who, sir, makes the trader? Who is most to blame? The enlightened, cultivated, intelligent man, who supports the system of which the trader is the inevitable result, or the poor trader himself? You make the public statement that calls for his trade, that **debauches** and **depraves** him, till he feels no shame in it; and in what are you better than he?*

Are you educated and he ignorant, you high and he low, you refined and he coarse, you talented and he simple?

In the day of a future Judgment, these very considerations may make it more tolerable for him than for you.

Mas'r: Master; form of address used by slaves when speaking to white men.

Embarrassed: Interfered with.

Property operations: Slave-trading business.

Ill-used man: One who has been abused or treated poorly.

Discontentedly: Without satisfaction.

Debauches: Corrupts or leads away from virtue.

Depraves: Perverts or corrupts morally.

Harriet Beecher Stowe, author of *Uncle Tom's Cabin*.

What happened next . . .

Readers all across the North were captivated by *Uncle Tom's Cabin*. The novel sold three hundred thousand copies in the first year following its publication, and went on to sell over two million copies in the next ten years. These sales made Stowe's work the best-selling book ever up to that time.

More importantly, *Uncle Tom's Cabin* raised people's awareness of the terrible injustice of slavery. It convinced countless Northerners to join the abolitionist movement. Some historians claim that, by making people in the North less willing to compromise on the issue of slavery, it helped cause the Civil War. In fact, President Abraham Lincoln once called Stowe "the little lady who wrote the book that made this big war."

Uncle Tom's Cabin also sold well in Europe and was translated into many foreign languages. Some historians have said that it helped persuade the leaders of England and France to remain neutral during the Civil War, rather than to support Confederate independence.

Of course, reaction in the Southern states was not so positive. Most people in the South were highly critical of the book. They claimed that Stowe distorted the facts of slavery and exaggerated the punishments that blacks received. "There never before was anything so detestable or so monstrous among women as this," wrote a reviewer for the *New Orleans Crescent*. Many states tried to ban the book, but Southerners still wanted to read it. In fact, copies sold so fast that bookstores in Charleston, South Carolina, could not keep up with demand.

Within the next few years, at least fifteen Southern writers published responses to *Uncle Tom's Cabin*. These books generally argued that blacks were better off under slavery in the South than they were living in poverty in the North. One Southern book that glorified slavery was called *Uncle Robin in His Cabin in Virginia and Tom without One in Boston.*

Did you know . . .

- The term "Uncle Tom" is still used today, although its meaning has changed a great deal over the years. The main character in Stowe's book is a gentle, patient, deeply religious man. His faith helps him to accept the hardships of slavery, because he believes that he will find a better life in heaven. During the second half of the 1800s, *Uncle Tom's Cabin* became the basis for a form of entertainment known as "Tom Shows." In some of these shows, white performers painted their faces and imitated black people while singing songs and doing skits. The Uncle Tom character who appeared in these shows was so docile (meek) and subservient (submissive) that he humiliated himself. Over time, "Uncle Tom" came to be used as a negative term for a black person who is overly eager to gain the acceptance of whites.

For Further Reading

Campbell, Stanley W. *The Slave Catchers: Enforcement of the Fugitive Slave Law 1850–1860.* Chapel Hill: University of North Carolina Press, 1970.

Kolchin, Peter. *American Slavery, 1619–1877.* New York: Hill and Wang, 1993.

Stampp, Kenneth M. *The Peculiar Institution: Slavery in the Ante-Bellum South.* New York: Knopf, 1956. Reprint, New York: Vintage Books, 1989.

Theodore Upson

Excerpt from Journal of Theodore Upson
Written in April 1861; originally published in 1943

A family's reaction to the start of the Civil War

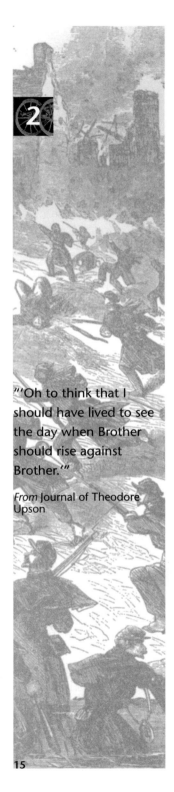

The Confederate attack on the Federal stronghold of Fort Sumter in April 1861 marked the beginning of the Civil War. The Confederate capture of Sumter made it clear that, after years of dark threats and bitter debate, the differences between the North and South would be settled on the battlefield.

At first, many people in both regions expressed great enthusiasm for the coming war. Big rallies and celebrations erupted in many major cities, as community leaders and ordinary citizens alike showed their patriotic spirit. This high level of support for the war was due in part to the long years of angry disagreement between America's Northern and Southern states. Their clashes over such issues as slavery and states' rights (the belief that each state has the right to decide how to handle various issues for itself without interference from the national government) had caused many Southerners and Northerners to dislike one another.

As James Stokesbury wrote in *A Short History of the Civil War,* hostility and cultural differences between the North and South led both regions to develop distorted views of the other region's populace. By the early 1860s, millions of

"'Oh to think that I should have lived to see the day when Brother should rise against Brother.'"

From Journal of Theodore Upson

Northerners had come to believe that "the typical Southern male was a hard-drinking, hard-riding wastrel [lazy person], living off the sweat of the slave, stated Stokesbury. [The Southern male was] boastful, bullying, threatening, fiscally and morally irresponsible, at best a romantic fool and at worst a sadistic [getting pleasure from physically or emotionally hurting others] beast." Many Northerners had also come to believe that Southern threats of secession (withdrawing) from the Union were nothing more than bluffs (misleading acts). Southerners, meanwhile, adopted a view of the Northerner as a "mean-spirited, hypocritical, money-grubbing capitalist, whining about the poor black slaves while keeping his own workers in conditions worse than slavery, determined to grind the South down through tariffs [taxes on imported goods] and to have his own way with the nation."

These foolish generalizations led many citizens in the North and South to view themselves as morally and physically superior to their foes. Northerners tended to view themselves as smart and mature and responsible, especially when compared to the people of the South. Many Southerners, meanwhile, believed that Southern culture had created generations of men and women who were more courageous, religious, and honorable than their counterparts in the North. These beliefs contributed to the excitement that many Americans felt about the war in its early days. After all, people in the North and the South had become used to the idea that they were superior to people in the other region. These feelings of superiority made each side confident that they would whip the other without too much difficulty.

Not all Americans believed in these stereotypes (oversimplified generalizations about a person, group, or issue) of each other and their countrymen, however. Many people in both the North and the South recognized that men and women of intelligence, courage, and integrity lived throughout America, not just in one region or the other. Not surprisingly, people from one section who had friends and relatives who lived in the other region were most likely to admit this.

In the days following the Confederate attack on Fort Sumter, U.S. president Abraham Lincoln (1809–1865) and Confederate president Jefferson Davis (1808–1889) both launched major efforts to strengthen their respective armies.

As the two governments proclaimed their need for soldiers, countless friends and families were torn apart by conflicting loyalties. Fiercely pro-Union families in the North went into mourning because they knew that sons and daughters and friends living in the South would probably pledge their loyalty to the Confederacy. Similarly, many pro-Confederacy families living in the South were crushed when they learned that sons or uncles or cousins who had married Northern women or found work in the North had decided to fight for the Union.

The arrival of the Civil War also forced soldiers in the U.S. Army to decide whether to remain a part of the Federal (Union) Army or resign to join the Confederacy. Most soldiers from the North retained their membership in the Federal military in order to help do their part in restoring the Union. But soldiers who hailed from Southern states faced a far more difficult choice. They were forced to choose between standing with their families and birth states or standing with the national government to which they had sworn loyalty.

George Henry Thomas chose to fight for the Union despite having been raised in Virginia. *(Photograph by Mathew Brady. Courtesy of the Library of Congress.)*

Southerners who chose to remain loyal to the Union often experienced great personal pain, as friends and family members condemned them for their decision. For example, George Henry Thomas (1816–1870) decided to fight for the Union even though he had been raised in Virginia. He went on to become one of the Union's top commanders, performing heroically at the Battle of Chickamauga (Georgia) and elsewhere. But Thomas's bravery did not matter to his sisters in Virginia, who refused to speak to him ever again. Another military veteran who chose to fight for the Union was navy commander Charles Steedman, a native of South Carolina. When Steedman publicly announced his loyalty to the Union, his brother James responded with a letter in which he called Charles "a Traitor to his Mother County . . . where lie

Two Virginia Brothers Become Enemies`

As hostilities grew between America's Northern and Southern regions, many families became divided as members chose opposite sides in the conflict. The Welsh brothers of Virginia, for example, became bitter enemies as a result of the war. James Welsh had grown up in Virginia's Shenandoah Valley. But he moved north to Illinois in the early 1850s, and by 1860 he had become a supporter of Abraham Lincoln. His brother John, however, remained in Virginia.

When John learned that his brother had voted for Lincoln in the 1860 presidential election, he wrote him a harsh letter in which he voiced his support for secession and stated how disappointed he was to find "that I have a brother who would advocate sending men here to butcher his own friends and relations." He went on to tell James that by joining the Republican Party, he showed his willingness to "sacrifice" his "home, mother, father, and brothers" for "the dear nigger."

Hurt and angered by his brother's outburst, James responded with his own letter. In this letter, he stated that he never dreamed that a brother of his would ever "raise a hand to tear down the glorious Stars and Stripes, a flag that we have been taught from our cradle to look on with pride. . . . I would strike down my own brother if he dare to raise a hand to destroy that flag. We have to rise in our might as a free independent nation and demand that law must and shall be respected or we shall find ourselves wiped from the face of the earth . . . and the principles of free government will be dashed to the ground forever."

After exchanging these two bitter letters, James and John Walsh never wrote or spoke to one another again. James Walsh enlisted in the North's Seventy-eighth Illinois regiment. During his term of service in the Union Army, he fought in several battles and participated in the famous 1864 march through Georgia, led by General William T. Sherman (1820–1891). After the war ended, he returned to Illinois. His brother, meanwhile, enlisted in the South's Twenty-seventh Virginia regiment. John Walsh served in the rebel army for two years before being killed at the Battle of Gettysburg.

the bones of his Father, Mother, & many dear relatives. [How could] a Brother in whose veins flows the same blood, Southern, true Southern . . . ever allow Northern principles to contaminate his pure soul?"

Wartime divisions between families and friends took place all over the country, but were particularly common in the geographic border states. These states—Missouri, Tennessee, Kentucky, Virginia, and Maryland—were geographically located in the center of the country, between the North and the South. They supported slavery, but also contained many people who were fiercely pro-Union in their views. In addition, these states and other nearby regions like the Kansas Territory and southern Indiana and Illinois featured populations with roots in both the North and South.

As the people who lived in these communities decided whether to support the Union or the Confederacy, countless individuals met with harsh words or tears when they informed their families and friends of their decision. "Throughout the border and middle states, tragic scenes took place as families were split, in many cases never to be reunited," wrote Stokesbury. "For what we consider as entities—this state or that state—were in reality thousands of agonizing individual choices, as men and women argued and prayed to discover their rightful path and place."

News of the rebel attack on Fort Sumter, then, sparked very different reactions across the country. In many homes and cities, people engaged in patriotic celebrations and white men rushed to enlist in the gathering armies. Some of these young enlistees—whether from the North or the South—were so confident that their side would roll to a grand and glorious victory that they worried that the war would end before they got a chance to see battle. But in some farmhouses and small communities, reaction to the news of the coming war triggered anguish and heartache. In these places, people recognized that the Civil War would pit family members, friends, and neighbors against one another on the field of battle.

Theodore Upson was a member of an Indiana farming household that greeted the news of the attack on Fort Sumter with great sorrow. His family knew that the coming war would probably pit them against friends and relatives who had built lives for themselves in the South. Upson was just a youngster when the Civil War broke out in the spring of 1861. But even though he could not enlist, he thought a great deal about what it would be like to go into battle against a Confederate Army that might include people he knew. Upson shared these thoughts in a personal journal that he kept. In the following excerpt, he recalls his family's reaction upon hearing the news that the war had begun.

Things to remember while reading the excerpt from the *Journal of Theodore Upson:*

- Upson's journal entries make it clear that many of his neighbors were eager to enlist. This was a common reaction in both regions of the divided nation. In fact, the secession of Southern states and the rebel capture of Fort Sumter triggered a great wave of army-building by both the Union and the Confederacy. In the South, existing state militias rushed to join the Confederate Army, while in the North, volunteers flooded Union recruiting stations when President Lincoln issued his request for seventy-five thousand military enlistees. This eagerness to volunteer for military service continued in both regions throughout 1861 and much of 1862. But as the war dragged on and casualty lists grew depressingly long, both governments were forced to resort to military drafts to maintain their armies.

- The Upson family's neighbors were very confident of a Union victory. When the Civil War began, many people in both the North and South thought that the war would end quickly, with their side victorious. But the Upsons and other people who had friends and relatives living in the enemy region were more likely to recognize that the war was going to bring great pain and sorrow to the nation.

- Upson's journal entries show how many communities in the South and the North developed stereotypical (too generalized) impressions about one another. Southerners viewed Northerners as greedy weaklings, while Northerners came to see people from the South as boastful and simple minded. These characterizations led both regions to underestimate the fighting spirit and determination of the other side.

Excerpt from Journal of Theodore Upson

Father and I were husking out some corn. . . . When William Cory came across the field (he had been down after the mail) he was excited and said, "Jonathan the **Rebs** have fired upon and taken Fort Sumpter [sic]." Father got white and couldn't say a word.

William said, "The President will fix them. He has called for 75,000 men and is going to **blocade** their ports, and just as soon as those fellows find out that the North means business they will get down off their high horse."

Father said little. We did not finish the crop and drove to the barn. Father left me to unload and put out the team [of horses] and went to the house. After I had finished I went in to dinner. Mother said, "What is the matter with Father?" He had gone right upstairs. I told her what we had heard. She went to him. After a while they came down. Father looked ten years older.

We sat down to the table. Grandma wanted to know what was the trouble. Father told her and she began to cry. "Oh my poor children in the South! Now they will suffer! God knows how they will suffer! I knew it would come! Jonathan I told you it would come!"

"They can come here and stay," said Father.

"No they will not do that. [The South] is their home. There they will stay. Oh to think that I should have lived to see the day when Brother should rise against Brother."

She and mother were crying and I lit out for the barn. I do hate to see women cry.

We had another meeting at the school house last night; we are raising money to take care of the families of those who enlist. A good many gave money, others **subscribed.** The Hulper boys have enlisted and Steve Lampman and some others. I said I would go but they laughed at me and said they wanted men not boys for this job; that it would all be over soon; that those fellows down South were big bluffers and would rather talk than fight. I am not so sure about that. I know the Hale boys would fight with [their] fists at any rate and I believe they would fight with guns too if needs be. I remember how Charlie [Hale] would get on our Dick [a horse] and ride on a **galop** across our south field cutting **mullin** heads with his wooden sword playing they were Indians or Mexicans (his father was in the Mexican War), and he looked fine. To be sure there was no danger but I feel pretty certain he could fight. May be it won't be such a picnic as some say it will. There has been a fight down in Virginia at Big Bethel. Al Beecher's Nephew was in it and wrote to his Uncle and he read the letter in his store. I could not make out which side whipped but from

Rebs: Rebels or Confederates.

Blocade: Blockade.

Subscribed: Pledged or promised to give money.

Galop: Gallop.

Mullin: Mullein; a type of plant.

Baseball Legend Abner Doubleday Fights at Fort Sumter

According to American legend, Abner Doubleday (1819–1893) was the inventor of the sport of baseball. As a nineteen-year-old cadet at the West Point Military Academy in New York in 1839, Doubleday allegedly devised the basic rules of the game. His rules included use of a diamond-shaped field and nine-player teams. But while generations of Americans have grown up believing that Doubleday invented baseball in 1839, historians believe that he did not really do so. In fact, it has been proven that a children's game similar to baseball existed long before Doubleday attended West Point.

But even though Abner Doubleday did not really invent baseball, he is still a notable figure in American history. After all, Doubleday was second in command at Fort Sumter when it came under attack from Confederate forces on April 12, 1861. As chief lieutenant for Major Robert Anderson (1805–1871), Doubleday took a leading role in defending the fort from the assault. The following entry from Doubleday's journal, *Reminiscences of Forts Sumter and Moultrie,* recalls how the fort finally fell into Confederate hands after long hours of cannon fire:

> Showers of [cannon]balls . . . poured into the fort in one incessant [unending] stream, causing great flakes of masonry to fall in all directions. When the immense mortar shells, after sailing high in the air, came down in a vertical direction and buried themselves in the parade ground, their explosion shook the fort like an earthquake. . . .
>
> At 10 A.M. [on April 13] a mortar shell passed through the roof and lodged in the flooring of the second story, where it burst and started the flames afresh. This too was extinguished, but the hot shots soon followed each other so rapidly that it was impossible for us to contend with them any longer. . . .
>
> By 11 A.M. the conflagration [fire] was terrible and disastrous. One fifth of the fort was on fire, and the wind drove the smoke in dense masses into the angle where we had all taken refuge. It seemed impossible to escape suffocation. Some lay down close to the ground, with handkerchiefs over their mouths, and others posted themselves near the embrasures [small openings in a wall through which to fire rifles], where the smoke was somewhat lessened by the draught of air. Every one suffered severely. . . .

the papers I think the Rebels had the best of it. Mother had a letter from the Hales. Charlie and his Father are in [their] army and Dayton wanted to go but was too young. I wonder if I were in our army and they should meet me would they shoot me. I suppose they would.

Abner Doubleday. *(Photograph by Mathew Brady. Courtesy of the Library of Congress.)*

Our fighting having ceased and the enemy being very jubilant, I thought it would be as well to show them that we were not all dead yet, and ordered the gunners to fire a few rounds more. I heard afterward that the enemy loudly cheered Anderson for his persistency under such adverse [difficult] circumstances.

The scene at this time was really terrific. The roaring and crackling of the flames, the dense masses of whirling smoke, the bursting of the enemy's shells and our own which were exploding in the burning rooms, the crashing of the shot, and the sound of masonry falling in every direction, made the fort a pandemonium [a place of chaos and noise]. . . . About 12:48 P.M. the end of the flagstaff was shot down and the [American] flag fell. . . .

[After Anderson and his Union troops finally surrendered], it was decided that the evacuation [of the fort] should take place the next morning. . . . The population of the surrounding country poured into Charleston in vast multitudes to witness the humiliation of the United States flag. We slept soundly that night for the first time, after all the fatigue and excitement of the two preceding days.

After leaving Fort Sumter, Doubleday continued to serve in the Union Army. He fought at some of the Civil War's greatest battles during the next few years, including the clashes at Antietam, Fredericksburg, Chancellorsville, and Gettysburg. After the war, he retired from the military at the rank of major general. Despite his brave performance during the Civil War, however, Doubleday remains best known as the "inventor" of the all-American game of baseball.

What happened next . . .

The Union and the Confederacy spent the first part of the summer of 1861 training and outfitting their ever-growing armies. This was a frustrating process at times. As James M. McPherson wrote in *Ordeal by Fire*, "seldom has a country been less prepared for a major war than the United States was in 1861."

Union major general Irvin McDowell. *(Courtesy of the National Archives and Records Administration.)*

When Fort Sumter fell in April 1861, neither the North nor the South had an army of any significant size or ability. And while Union and Confederate calls for military volunteers quickly increased the size of the two sides' armies, the governments struggled mightily to mold these inexperienced men into good soldiers. Both governments scrambled to find qualified military officers to train the thousands of new enlistees. In addition, efforts to provide their respective armies with rifles, uniforms, and other supplies sometimes got sidetracked by shortages of materials and political corruption.

These frantic efforts to build disciplined armies in a matter of weeks were doomed to failure. As the primary Union Army gathered around the capital city of Washington, D.C., some of President Lincoln's advisors warned that the Union's inexperienced troops would need months of training before they would be ready to go to war against the South. But other officials were very confident of victory, and many Northern communities showed great impatience at the idea of waiting to attack the rebel states of the Confederacy. This belief in a quick and decisive Union victory was encouraged by many Northern newspapers. The *New York Times* predicted that the Confederacy would be destroyed within thirty days, and many other Northern newspapers expressed similar confidence.

Of course, Southern citizens and newspaper editors made equally foolish claims about the outcome of the upcoming war. Editorials in newspapers in Richmond, Atlanta, and other Southern cities boasted that the Union Army did not have a chance of defeating the Confederate forces. Ordi-

nary soldiers felt this way, too. Many Southerners claimed, for example, that one rebel soldier could whip ten Northerners. As one Confederate infantryman boasted, "The Yankee army is filled up with the scum of creation and ours with the best blood of the grand old Southland."

Swayed by minor Union victories in western Virginia and continued public pressure to soundly defeat the South, Lincoln ultimately approved a plan to attack a major Confederate camp located at Manassas Junction, Virginia, about thirty miles southwest of Washington. A Union army under the command of Irvin McDowell (1818–1885) promptly marched into Virginia, where it intended to join forces with another Union army. Confederate maneuvers prevented the two armies from joining, however.

On July 21, McDowell faced a smaller rebel army led by General Pierre G. T. Beauregard (1818–1893) at Manassas Junction, on the shores of the Bull Run River. As the two

Soldiers rest near a pontoon bridge at Bull Run River in Virginia. *(Courtesy of the National Archives and Records Administration.)*

Pierre G.T. Beauregard, whose small Confederate army faced Irvin McDowell's army at Manassas. *(Courtesy of the Library of Congress)*

armies prepared to fight, hundreds of people from Washington gathered on the hillsides above the river valley to watch. These observers were so certain of a Union victory that they brought picnic baskets and blankets with them to celebrate.

But the first major battle of the Civil War did not develop as the picnickers expected. When the two armies clashed, it was clear that both forces were inexperienced and undisciplined. Both sides fought hard, but most efforts to engage in strategic maneuvers fell apart in confusion and misunderstood orders. By the afternoon, McDowell's Union troops had gained an advantage. But rebel reinforcements led by General Joseph Johnston (1807–1891) turned the battle in favor of the South, and the First Battle of Bull Run (also sometimes known as the First Battle of Manassas) ended in a big Confederate victory.

The arrival of Johnston's troops helped Beauregard maintain his position at Manassas and triggered a Union retreat that broke up into panicky flight. Frightened picnickers rushed from the area as well, and the road back to Washington became clogged with a mixture of scared civilians and humiliated soldiers.

The Confederate triumph at Manassas increased Southern overconfidence in its military superiority. Southerners viewed the victory as evidence that they were better fighters than the Union soldiers, even though more Confederates were killed or wounded in the battle. It also convinced many Southern communities that the North would soon give up its efforts to restore the Union.

In reality, though, the Union defeat at the First Battle of Bull Run jolted the North awake. The loss caused many Northerners to adopt a new outlook on the war. Dropping their view of the South as an easy target, they were forced to admit that those neighbors who saw the South as a dangerous foe were right. But instead of giving up, as the South expected, Northern communities expressed renewed dedication to the Union cause. "A mood of grim determination replaced the incandescent [brightly shining] optimism of the spring," wrote James M. McPherson in *Ordeal by Fire*. "If Southerners thought the Yankees would quit after one licking, they soon learned differently."

Did you know . . .

- The Civil War is sometimes called "the Brothers' War." It acquired this name in part because it divided so many American families, and also because it set countrymen against one another on the field of battle.

- Four brothers of Mary Todd Lincoln (1818–1882)—the wife of President Abraham Lincoln—fought on behalf of the South in the Civil War. In addition, three of her brothers-in-law fought under the Confederate flag, and one of them rose to the rank of general in the rebel army.

- Kentucky senator John J. Crittenden (1787–1863) was one of many fathers who experienced the anguish of seeing their sons fight on opposite sides of the Civil War. One of his two sons became a general in the Union Army, while the other rose to the rank of general in the Confederate Army.

- Fort Sumter was named a national monument in 1948. National monuments are natural landmarks, structures, or historic sites that are preserved by the U.S. government for future generations of citizens to study and enjoy. American national monuments are managed by the National Park Service.

- Confederate general Pierre G. T. Beauregard, who led the South to victory at the First Battle of Bull Run, was the same man who led the successful assault on Fort Sumter that marked the beginning of the Civil War. A native of Louisiana, Beauregard resigned his position as superintendent of the U.S. Military Academy at West Point in order to join the Confederate Army.

For Further Reading

McPherson, James M. *For Cause and Comrades: Why Men Fought in the Civil War.* New York: Oxford University Press, 1997.

Meredith, Roy. *Storm Over Sumter.* New York: Simon & Schuster, 1957.

Mitchell, Reid. *The Vacant Chair: The Northern Soldier Leaves Home.* New York: Oxford University Press, 1993.

Potter, David M. *The Impending Crisis, 1848–1861.* New York: Harper & Row, 1976.

Stokesbury, James. *A Short History of the Civil War.* New York: Morrow, 1995.

Upson, Theodore Frelinghuysen. *With Sherman to the Sea; the Civil War Letters, Diaries & Reminiscences of Theodore F. Upson.* Baton Rouge: Louisiana State University Press, 1943. Reprint, Bloomington: Indiana University Press, 1958.

Frederick Douglass

Excerpt from "The American Apocalypse"
Speech delivered in Rochester, New York, on June 16, 1861

*An abolitionist argues that a Union
with slavery is not worth saving*

When the Civil War began in 1861, President Abraham Lincoln (1809–1865) and many other people in the North claimed that the conflict was not about slavery. Instead, they said that the North was fighting in order to preserve the United States as one nation. "My paramount [primary] aim in this struggle is to save the Union, and is not either to save or destroy slavery," Lincoln stated. "If I could save the Union without freeing any slaves, I would do it, and if I could save it by freeing all the slaves I would do it; and if I could save it by freeing some and leaving others alone I would also do that."

Lincoln chose preserving the Union as his primary war aim partly for political reasons. He did not want to risk losing the support of the four "border" states—Delaware, Kentucky, Maryland, and Missouri—that allowed slavery but remained loyal to the United States. Another reason that people claimed the war was not about slavery was widespread racism. Even in the North, many white people believed that they were superior to blacks. Therefore, they did not feel strongly about ending slavery.

"For the statesman of this hour to permit any settlement of the present war between slavery and freedom, which will leave untouched and undestroyed the relation of master and slave, would not only be a great crime, but a great mistake, the bitter fruit of which would poison the life blood of unborn generations."

Harriet Tubman: The Nation Must Kill Slavery before Slavery Kills the Nation

Harriet Tubman (1820–1913) was a fugitive slave who helped other slaves gain their freedom through the Underground Railroad. The Underground Railroad was not actually a railroad. It was a secret network of abolitionists who helped slaves escape from their masters and settle in the Northern United States and Canada. The Underground Railroad system consisted of a chain of homes and barns known as "safe houses" or "depots." The people who helped the runaway slaves go from one safe house to the next were known as "conductors." Tubman made nineteen dangerous trips into slave territory as a conductor and helped more than three hundred slaves gain their freedom.

Like Frederick Douglass, Tubman believed that slavery harmed the entire United States. She thought that the only way for the North to win the war and preserve the Union was to abolish slavery. In the following passage, Tubman uses an animal story to express her feelings about President Lincoln's war policies. The snake represents slavery, and the person bitten by the snake represents the Union. Through the story, Tubman shows that slavery has caused dangerous problems for the nation in the past, and will continue to do so unless it is wiped out.

Harriet Tubman. (Reproduced by permission of The Granger Collection.)

God won't let Master Lincoln beat the South until he does the right thing. Master Lincoln, he's a great man, and I'm a poor Negro, but this Negro can tell Master Lincoln how to save money and young men. He can do it by setting the Negroes free. Suppose there was an awful big snake down there on the floor. He bites you. Folks all scared, because you may die. You send for the doctor to cut the bite; but the snake is rolled up there, and while doctor is doing it, he bites you again. The doctor cuts out that bite; but while he's doing it, the snake springs up and bites you again, and so he keeps doing it, till you kill him. That's what Master Lincoln ought to know.

In reality, the dispute between the North and the South involved a number of different issues, including the question of how much power should be granted to the individual states and how much should be held by the federal government. But slavery was the one issue upon which the two sides could not compromise. When the Southern states seceded from (left) the Union, they made it clear that their main goal was to defend their way of life, which depended on the "peculiar institution" of slavery. For this reason, Northern abolitionists (people who worked to put an end to slavery) and free blacks argued that the real issue behind the war was slavery. They did not believe that Lincoln could preserve the Union without destroying slavery. They wanted Northern political leaders to make abolishing slavery the main purpose of the Civil War.

Frederick Douglass (c. 1818–1895) was one of the leaders in the debate over the North's war aims. Douglass had escaped from slavery in 1838. Over the next few years, he became a prominent member of the abolitionist movement. He wrote many books and articles, and spoke about his experiences as a slave throughout the North and in Europe. "He stood before packed auditoriums and testified [declared] as to what it was like to be a slave in America," Louis P. Masur wrote in *The Real War Will Never Get in the Books: Selections from Writers during the Civil War.* "He stood before huge congregations and pleaded for equality and justice for the black race."

As soon as the war started, Douglass began criticizing Lincoln's war policies. He pressured the president to make emancipation (granting freedom from slavery or oppression) the North's main priority in the war. In one editorial, Douglass argued that by fighting about secession rather than slavery, "we strike at the effect, and leave the cause unharmed." The following excerpt comes from one of many speeches Douglass made shortly after the start of the Civil War. He outlines some of the negative effects slavery had on the basic principles of the country, and argues that the Union is not worth saving if it allows slavery.

Things to remember while reading Frederick Douglass's "American Apocalypse" speech:
- At the time Douglass became famous as a writer and speaker, many white people believed that black people were inferior. They created a stereotype (an overly simpli-

fied concept or belief about a group of people) of black people as uneducated and unable to express intelligent thoughts or opinions. But when they were exposed to the speeches and writings of black people like Frederick Douglass, many whites were forced to admit that those beliefs were wrong.

- Before the Civil War started, supporters of slavery in the Southern states took many steps to ensure that the institution would continue to exist in the United States. For example, they pushed to extend slavery to new states and territories in the West. In this way, they hoped to gain proslavery representatives in the U.S. Congress so that no new antislavery laws would be passed. Many Southern states also banned (prohibited) the sale of written materials that opposed slavery, such as the famous novel *Uncle Tom's Cabin* by Harriet Beecher Stowe (1811–1896). Douglass mentions some of these Southern tactics (methods) in his speech. He argues that these measures are inconsistent with the values set forth in the Constitution. He claims that the Southerners will erode the basic freedoms of all Americans if they are not stopped. "Freedom of the speech, of the press, of education, of labor, of locomotion, and indeed all kinds of freedom, are felt to be a standing menace [threat] to slavery," he explains. Since Douglass believed that slavery was poisoning the country, he felt that the only way to save the Union was to abolish slavery.

Excerpt from "The American Apocalypse" speech by Frederick Douglass

Beget: Produce or cause.

Dominion: Absolute authority or power.

Repose: Lie peacefully.

Rectitude: Moral correctness.

*Slavery, like all other gross and powerful forms of wrong which appear directly to human pride and selfishness, when once admitted into the framework of society, has the ability and tendency to **beget** a character in the whole network of society surrounding it, favorable to its continuance. The very law of its existence is growth and **dominion**. Natural and harmonious relations easily **repose** in their own **rectitude**, while all such as are false and unnatural are conscious of their own weakness, and must seek strength from* without. Hence the explanation of the uneasy, restless, eager anxiety of slaveholders. Our history shows that from the formation of this Government, until the attempt now making to break it up, this class of men have been constantly pushing schemes for the safety and supremacy of their own class system. They have had marvelous success. They have completely destroyed freedom in the slave States, and were doing their best to accomplish the same in the free States. He is a very imperfect **reasoner** who attributes the steady rise and **ascendancy** of slavery to anything else than the nature of slavery itself. Truth may repose upon its **inherent** strength, but a falsehood rests for support upon external **props**. Slavery is the most **stupendous** of all lies, and depends for existence upon a favorable adjustment of all its surroundings. Freedom of the speech, of the press, of education, of labor, of locomotion, and indeed all kinds of freedom, are felt to be a standing **menace** to slavery. Hence, the friends of slavery are **bounded** by the necessity of their system to do just what the history of the country shows they have done—that is, to seek to **subvert** all liberty, and to prevent all the safeguards of human rights. They could not do otherwise. It was the controlling law of their situation.

Now, if these views be sound, and are borne out by the whole history of American slavery, then for the statesman of this hour to permit any settlement of the present war between slavery and freedom, which will leave untouched and undestroyed the relation of master and slave, would not only be a great crime, but a great mistake, the bitter fruit of which would poison the life blood of unborn generations. No grander opportunity was ever given to any nation to **signalize**, either its justice and humanity, or its intelligence and statesmanship, than is now given to the loyal American people. We are brought to a point in our National career where two roads meet and **divert**. It is the critical moment for us. The destiny of the mightiest Republic in the modern world hangs upon the decision of that hour. If our Government shall have the wisdom to see, and the nerve to act, we are safe. If it fails, we perish, and go to our own place with those **nations of antiquity** long blotted from the maps of the world. I have only one voice, and that is neither loud nor strong. I speak to but few, and have little influence; but whatever I am or may be, I may, at such a time as this, in the name of justice, liberty and humanity, and in that of the permanent security and welfare of the whole nation, urge all men, and especially the Government, to the **abolition** of slavery. Not a slave should be left a slave in the returning footprints of the American army gone to put down this

Reasoner: Person who thinks or reasons.

Ascendancy: Superior importance or influence.

Inherent: Basic or essential.

Props: Devices used to keep something standing.

Stupendous: Astonishingly great.

Menace: Threat or danger.

Bounded: Limited or confined.

Subvert: Corrupt or undermine.

Signalize: Point out or make clear.

Divert: Turn in different directions.

Nations of antiquity: Countries that existed in ancient times.

Abolition: Destruction or elimination.

Sound: Sensible or correct.

Liberation: Granting of freedom.

*slaveholding rebellion. **Sound** policy, not less than humanity, demands the instant **liberation** of every slave in the rebel States.*

What happened next . . .

The North's war aims gradually changed to include freeing the slaves as well as restoring the Union. Although the arguments made by Douglass and other abolitionists helped make this change possible, other factors were probably more important. For example, Lincoln and other Northern leaders came to see the practical, military benefits that they could gain through emancipation. The Confederate Army used slaves to perform hard labor during the war. The slaves built forts and dug trenches, transported artillery and unloaded shipments of arms, and set up army camps and acted as cooks and servants for the soldiers. Slave labor gave the South an advantage by enabling more white men to join the fight. Northern leaders began to realize that freeing the slaves would help the Union win the war.

Once the Civil War began, thousands of slaves took the opportunity to escape from the South. They came into Union Army camps and served as laborers, scouts, and spies for the Northern war effort. Union officials developed a policy that allowed the army to take away any Southern property that was used in the Confederate war effort as "contraband of war." Since slaves were considered property in the South, escaped slaves were allowed to remain in the North. In August 1861, the U.S. Congress passed the first of two Confiscation Acts, which made the contraband policy into law. President Lincoln finally freed the slaves on January 1, 1863, with his Emancipation Proclamation.

Frederick Douglass remained outspoken during the remainder of the Civil War. Once freeing the slaves became a Northern war aim, he argued that black men should be allowed to join the Union Army and fight for the liberation of their race. After the Union Army accepted black soldiers in 1862, Douglass took a leading role in convincing free blacks in the North to volunteer. In fact, two of his sons served in the famous Fifty-Fourth Massachusetts regiment. When black soldiers faced discrimination in the army, Douglass helped them get paid the same wages as white soldiers of the same rank. After the war ended, he continued fighting for blacks to receive equal rights in American society. "In many ways [Douglass] was the conscience of the nation," according to William C. Davis, Brian C. Pohanka, and Don Troiani in *Civil War Journal: The Leaders.* "He kept before the country the idea that this was a war, not just to bring the nation back together, but it was a war to end slavery, to bring equality to black people, and to make them part of American society."

Outspoken black leader Frederick Douglass.

Did you know . . .

- Learning to read and write gave Douglass the means to escape slavery. As a boy, he lived on a Maryland plantation owned by Hugh Auld. Auld's wife taught Douglass to read from the Bible. "From that moment I understood the pathway from slavery to freedom," he recalled. "It was just what I wanted and I got it at a time when I least expected it." Later, Douglass tricked the white children of the plantation into sharing their books and homework assignments with him. Most Southern whites made every effort to prevent slaves from obtaining an education. They believed that uneducated slaves would calmly accept their condition. They worried that slaves who learned to read would gain a greater awareness of the world around them and become dissatisfied with their lives. Douglass eventually turned his writing and speaking ability into a career as a prominent abolitionist. Throughout his life, he always maintained that other black men and women could achieve great things if they were given education and opportunity.

Abolotionist William Lloyd Garrison. *(Courtesy of the Library of Congress.)*

• After escaping from slavery in 1838, Douglass became interested in the growing abolitionist movement. In 1841, he went to hear famous abolitionist William Lloyd Garrison (1805–1879) speak in Nantucket, Massachusetts. When Garrison learned that there was a fugitive slave in the audience, he asked Douglass to say a few words. Douglass kept the audience on the edge of their seats for two hours telling stories about his life as a slave. He became an overnight sensation in the antislavery movement. "The public had itching ears to hear a colored man speak and particularly a slave," one abolitionist stated.

• As Douglass became famous as an abolitionist writer and speaker, his life became more dangerous. He was still a fugitive slave. His former master knew where he was and could send a slave catcher after him at any time. To avoid returning to slavery, Douglass went to England—where slavery was outlawed—in 1845. While he was there, his friends in the United States arranged to purchase him from his owner. He thus returned to the United States two years later as a free man.

For Further Reading

Blight, David W. *Frederick Douglass' Civil War: Keeping Faith in Jubilee.* Baton Rouge: Louisiana State University Press, 1989.

Friedheim, William. *Freedom's Unfinished Revolution: An Inquiry into the Civil War and Reconstruction.* New York: New Press, 1996.

Harding, Vincent. *There Is a River: The Black Struggle for Freedom in America.* New York: Harcourt, 1981.

Huggins, Nathan. *Slave and Citizen: The Life of Frederick Douglass.* Boston: Little, Brown, 1980.

McFeely, William S. *Frederick Douglass.* New York: Norton, 1991.

McPherson, James M. *The Negro's Civil War: How American Negroes Felt and Acted During the War for the Union.* New York: Pantheon, 1965. Reprint, Urbana: University of Illinois Press, 1982.

Frank Holsinger

Excerpt from "How Does One Feel Under Fire?"
Covering events from 1862; first published in 1898

A soldier writes about his fears on the battlefield

During the course of the American Civil War, approximately 620,000 soldiers (360,000 Union and 260,000 Confederate) lost their lives. As these troops died, surviving soldiers struggled to conquer their fears and conduct themselves with honor. Most soldiers believed in the cause for which they were fighting, and many entered the war in order to prove their manhood. But even the bravest of men sometimes found it difficult to continue fighting when friends and comrades were falling all around them.

Many factors influenced a soldier's performance in battle. Certainly, individual beliefs and motives could have a big impact on a soldier's behavior while under fire. For example, Union soldiers who were fiercely devoted to the cause of abolitionism (putting an end to slavery) or restoration (a return to a former condition) of the Union sometimes went into battle more willingly than comrades who did not feel the same way. Similarly, Confederate soldiers who believed strongly in the South's right to secede from (leave) the Union showed a great willingness to go into battle in order to defend that right. The deaths of friends and loved ones also affected

"The worst condition to endure is when you fall wounded upon the field. Now you are helpless. No longer are you filled with the enthusiasm of battle. You are helpless—the bullets still fly over and about you—you no longer are able to shift your position or seek shelter. Every bullet as it strikes near you is a new terror."

the battle-readiness of individual soldiers. Some men felt a greater reluctance to go into battle after witnessing the death of a good friend or learning of the death of a brother. Others, though, rushed into combat in order to take revenge on the enemy. In fact, hatred of the enemy became a major motivation for thousands of soldiers during the later stages of the war.

Still, countless Civil War diaries and journals make it clear that no matter what their motivation was, soldiers on both sides always struggled with fear. "I don't pretend to say I wasn't afraid," stated one Union officer who fought at the Battle of Antietam in western Maryland in 1862. "And I must say that I did not see a face but that turned pale or hear a voice that did not tremble." A veteran Confederate officer confessed similar emotions. "[I am always] *badly scared.* . . . I am not as brave as I thought I was. I never wanted out of a place as bad in my life." Nonetheless, many soldiers were even more scared of being viewed as a coward. Determined to avoid this shame, they marched into battle again and again.

Emotions of fear were often greatest in the minutes or hours before battle, when soldiers wondered if they would survive to eat another meal or see another sunrise. During this time of growing tension, each soldier struggled to stay calm. But few soldiers felt comfortable discussing their fears because of concerns that they would be treated as cowards. "Some Civil War soldiers [realized that] . . . courage is not the absence of fear but the mastery of it," wrote James M. McPherson in *For Cause and Comrades.* "Nevertheless, to admit fear openly, even to family or close friends, came hard for them." For many soldiers, this inability to talk about their fears increased their pre-battle anxiety to the point that they were actually relieved when combat began. The fighting gave them an opportunity to release the emotions and nervous energy they had bottled up inside.

Military leadership also had a major impact on the morale and emotions of soldiers. Both Union and Confederate troops were willing to fight under officers whom they respected. But their performance often declined if they did not like or respect their commanders. In fact, officers sometimes had to display special courage in order to keep the respect of their troops. "When once the troops lose confidence in the bravery of their Commander, they necessarily have an utter contempt for him," confirmed one Confederate soldier.

Soldiers who were treated badly or indifferently by their commanding officers were also less likely to perform at a high level on the field of battle. Both Union and Confederate troops resented receiving harsh punishments for minor rule violations. They also hated officers who took advantage of their status to secure good food and comfortable camp lodging at times when ordinary soldiers under their command were hungry and cold. "The two most important criteria for a good officer," wrote McPherson, "were concern for the welfare of his men and leadership by example—that is, personal courage and a willingness to do anything he asked his men to do."

The bodies of Confederate soldiers are gathered in preparation for burial. *(Courtesy of the Library of Congress.)*

Many military officers did show their men that they were willing to risk their lives in battle. In fact, as a percentage of total casualties, officers were killed more often than enlisted men. Approximately 8 percent of all Union generals who served in the Civil War were killed in battle, compared to less than 6 percent of all Union soldiers. In the Confederate army, 18 percent of all Confederate generals were killed in action, while only 12 percent of the entire rebel army died in battle.

Regiments often became fiercely devoted to officers who performed bravely in combat and showed concern for their troops. In fact, some young soldiers came to view their commanders as father figures. They worked and fought hard in order to gain the approval of their commanders, and felt a great sense of loss when these officers died. At times, these relationships also took a heavy toll on officers. Many commanders, for example, found it emotionally exhausting to order their soldiers into battles that were sure to claim some of their lives.

In most cases, soldiers who were ordered into battle managed to conquer their fears and doubts. Despite desperate periods of homesickness and the ever-present fear of being wounded or killed, they conducted themselves honorably. Sometimes, though, military officers had to resort to threats and various forms of punishment in order to make sure that troops followed orders to go into combat. Some army units used the threat of violence to force frightened soldiers forward, while others threatened reluctant troops with public humiliation. Most officers did not like to use such harsh measures. But they realized that entire regiments might fall into attitudes of panic or disobedience if such behavior was permitted.

Military success was another important factor in the performance and attitudes of Civil War soldiers. "Victory in battle pumped up their internal morale and gave them a more positive attitude toward the next battle," noted McPherson. "Defeat lowered morale and caused many soldiers to wonder whether it was worthwhile to continue risking their lives." Victories and defeats that soldiers experienced personally had the greatest impact on morale, of course. But the outcomes of distant battles often had a major impact on military morale, too. During periods of the war when the Confederacy seemed to be winning, for example, the letters and diaries of Union soldiers contained countless expressions of self-doubt and discouragement. Rebel troops, meanwhile, wrote excitedly about their victories and expressed optimism about securing independence for the Confederacy. But when the Union Army claimed a series of major victories in 1863 and 1864, excited Northern soldiers expressed new enthusiasm for the fight even as the morale of battered Confederate troops crumbled. "The soldiers are all discouraged," admitted one Confederate soldier after fighting in the Battle of Gettysburg in Pennsylvania in 1863. "And they dread the thoughts of meeting the yankees again & [losing their] lives in a cause they consider to be nearly hopeless."

Battlefield experience was another important factor in the military performance of many Civil War soldiers. Young recruits without any wartime experience often expressed great eagerness to prove themselves in battle. But when they actually faced enemy gunfire and heard the boom of enemy cannons, these "green" (inexperienced) soldiers sometimes became overwhelmed with fear and confusion. The sight of dead comrades and enemy soldiers also made many green recruits wonder how they could possibly survive the war. But as time passed, many of these soldiers learned how to control their fear and develop their military skills. These veteran (experienced) troops became the backbone of both the Union and Confederate armies.

Frank Holsinger was one of thousands of Civil War soldiers who wrote about their wartime fears and experiences in journals and letters to loved ones. A Union captain who commanded the Nineteenth U.S. Colored Infantry, Holsinger retired from the military at the end of the war with the brevet (honorary) rank of major. In the following excerpt from his journal, Holsinger writes about how it felt to be shot at and discussed the many factors that influenced soldier morale.

Things to remember while reading the excerpt from "How Does One Feel Under Fire?":

- A number of the experiences that Holsinger talks about took place at the Battle of Antietam in Maryland (September 1862), in which Union forces halted a major Confederate advance towards Pennsylvania. This one-day clash produced more casualties (twenty-three thousand) than any other single day of the war. In fact, historians note that more than twice as many Americans were killed or wounded at Antietam as in the War of 1812 (1812–15), the Mexican War (1846–48), and the Spanish-American War (1898) combined.

- Holsinger notes that Civil War battles were so violent and bloody that many soldiers wondered how they could possibly survive. In fact, many soldiers went into battle convinced that they would die within the next few hours. Despite these terrible feelings, though, thousands and thousands of brave Confederate and Union troops willingly marched into battle to fight for their cause.

- Holsinger relates one incident at Antietam in which General George Meade (1815–1872)—who would later lead Union forces to victory at Gettysburg—physically attacks a frightened soldier. Commanding officers did not like to

**Union major general George
G. Meade.** *(Courtesy of the
National Archives and Records
Administration.)*

resort to such measures, but they sometimes felt that they had no other choice. In fact, both armies eventually established special units that were ordered to prevent frightened soldiers from hanging back during a battle. These units were sometimes given orders to shoot troops who refused to join the fight.

• The atmosphere before major battles sometimes became almost unbearably tense for soldiers. During these periods, soldiers often imagined that they would soon be killed or suffer terrible, crippling injuries. Occasionally, soldiers would try to joke around as a way of relieving this pre-battle tension. "The nearer we are to the enemy the greater seems the inclination [tendency] to jest and merriment," one Confederate officer noted. Holsinger writes about one soldier who managed to lighten the mood within his unit by joking that the horribly violent battle ahead was mere "skirmishing" (a minor encounter or clash).

• As Holsinger confirms, experienced troops tended to perform much better in battle than soldiers who had never been under fire before. Inexperienced soldiers typically had very romantic ideas about war, and they sometimes became overwhelmed when they saw what war was really like. After being exposed to the war's violence and pain, however, soldiers improved their skills and reached a better understanding of the war's high cost. "I have seen enough of the glory of war," wrote one veteran soldier from Virginia. "I am sick of seeing dead men and men's limbs torn from their bodies."

Excerpt from "How Does One Feel Under Fire?"

The influence of a courageous man is most helpful in battle. Thus at Antietam, when surprised by the Sixth Georgia Regiment, lying immediately behind the fence at the celebrated cornfield, allowing our regiment to approach within thirty feet, and then pouring in a **volley** *that* **decimated** *our ranks fully one-half; the regiment was* **demoralized.** *I was worse—I was* **stampeded.** *I did not expect to stop this side of the Pennsylvania line. I met a tall, thin young soldier, very boyish in manner, but cool as a cucumber . . . who yelled: "Rally, boys, rally! Die like men; don't run like dogs!" Instantly all fear vanished. "Why can I not stand and take what this boy can?" I* **commenced** *loading and firing, and from this on I was as comfortable as I had been in more pleasant places.*

How natural it is for a man to suppose that if a gun is discharged, he or some one is sure to be hit. He soon finds, however, that the only damage done, in ninety-nine cases out of a hundred, the only thing killed is the powder! It is not infrequently that a whole line of battle (this among raw troops) will fire upon an advancing line, and no **perceptible** *damage* **ensue.** *They wonder how men can stand such treatment, when really they have done no damage save the terrific noise* **incident** *to the discharge. To undertake to say how many discharges are necessary to the death of a soldier in battle would be* **presumptuous,** *but I have frequently heard the remark that it took a man's weight in lead to kill him.*

In **presentiments** *of death I have no confidence. While I have seen men go into battle predicting truthfully their own death, yet I believe it is the belief of nine out of ten who go into battle that that is their last. I have never gone into battle that I did not expect to be killed. I have seen those who had no thought of death coming to them killed outright. Thus Corporal George Horton, wounded at South Mountain, wrapped his handkerchief around his wounded arm and carried the* **colors** *of our regiment to Antietam. Being asked why he did not make the best of it and go to the hospital, that he was liable to be killed, he answered, "The bullet has not [yet] been* **moulded** *to kill me." Alas! He was killed the next day.*

My **sensations** *at Antietam were a* **contradiction.** *When we were in line [passing through the woods],* the boom of cannon and

Volley: The firing of many weapons at the same time.

Decimated: Destroyed.

Demoralized: Depressed or without confidence.

Stampeded: Ran away in a panic.

Commenced: Began.

Perceptible: Noticeable.

Ensue: Immediately follow.

Incident: Related to.

Presumptuous: Excessively confident or arrogant.

Presentiments: Feelings that something is about to occur.

Colors: Flag.

Moulded: Made.

Sensations: Emotions.

Contradiction: Inconsistent.

Lodgment: Home or resting place.

Minies: Rifle bullets.

Sizzing: Streaking or shooting past.

Indefinable: Impossible to describe.

Cowers: Hides.

Tarry: Delay or linger.

Transaction: Event.

Panorama: Series of pictures showing the progression of a scene or event.

Unstrung: Jittery or nervous.

Galling: Irritating or bothersome.

Unfortunate: Unlucky soldier.

Listlessly: Showing little strength.

Pulsate: Beat.

Twang: Accent.

Infectious: Spreads to others.

Proposition: Situation.

Antagonists: Enemies.

Retire: Retreat.

Ecstasies: Supreme joy.

Resonant: Can be heard.

Spitefully: Angrily or with hostility.

the hurtling shell as it crashed through the trees or exploding found its **lodgment** in human flesh; the **minies sizzing** and savagely spotting the trees; the deathlike silence save the "steady men" of our officers. The shock to the nerves were **indefinable**—one stands, as it were, on the brink of eternity as he goes into action. One man alone steps from the ranks and **cowers** behind a large tree, his nerves gone; he could go no farther. General [George] Meade sees him, and, calling a sergeant, says, "Get that man in ranks." The sergeant responds, the man refuses; General Meade rushes up with, "I'll move him!" Whipping out his saber, he deals the man a blow, he falls—who he was, I do not know. The general has no time to **tarry** or make inquiries. A lesson to those witnessing the scene. The whole **transaction** was like that of a **panorama**. I felt at the time the action was cruel and needless on the part of the general. I changed my mind when I became an officer, when with sword and pistol drawn to enforce discipline by keeping my men in place when going into the conflict.

When the nerves are thus **unstrung**, I have known relief by a silly remark. Thus at Antietam, when in line of battle in front of the wood and exposed to a **galling** fire from the cornfield, standing waiting expectant with "What next?" the minies zipping by occasionally, one making the awful thud as it struck some **unfortunate**. As we thus stood **listlessly**, breathing a silent prayer, our hearts having ceased to **pulsate** or our minds on home and loved ones, expecting soon to be mangled or perhaps killed, some one makes an idiotic remark; thus at this time it is Mangle [one of the soldiers], in a high nasal **twang**, with "D——d sharp skirmishing in front." There is a laugh, it is **infectious**, and we are once more called back to life.

The battle when it goes your way is a different **proposition**. Thus having reached the east wood, each man sought a tree from behind which he not only sought protection, but dealt death to our **antagonists**. They halt, also seeking protection behind trees. They soon begin to **retire**, falling back into the cornfield. We now rush forward. We cheer; we are in **ecstasies**.

While shells and canister are still **resonant** and minies sizzing **spitefully**, yet I think this one of the supreme moments of my existence. . . .

The worst condition to endure is when you fall wounded upon the field. Now you are helpless. No longer are you filled with the enthusiasm of battle. You are helpless—the bullets still fly over and about you—you no longer are able to shift your position or seek shelter.

*Every bullet as it strikes near you is a new terror. **Perchance** you are enabled to take out your handkerchief, which you raise in **supplication** to the enemy to not fire in your direction and to your friends of your helplessness. This is a trying moment. How slowly time flies! Oh, the agony to the poor wounded man, who alone can ever know its horrors! Thus, at Bermuda Hundreds* [a Union base in southeastern Virginia], *November 28th, being in charge of the picket-line, we were attacked, which we **repulsed** and were rejoiced, yet the firing is main-*

Antietam bridge. *(Courtesy of the Library of Congress.)*

Perchance: Maybe.

Supplication: Begging or hoping for mercy.

Repulsed: Turned back.

tained. I am struck in the left forearm, though not disabled; soon I am struck in the right shoulder by an explosive bullet, which is imbedded in my shoulder-strap. We still maintain a spiteful fire. About [noon] I am struck again in my right forearm, which is broken and the main artery cut; soon we improvise a **tourniquet** by using a canteen-strap, and with a bayonet the **same** is twisted until blood ceases to flow. To retire is impossible, and for nine weary hours, or until late in the night, I remain on the line. I am alone with my thoughts; I think of home, of the seriousness of my condition; I see myself a cripple for life—perchance I may not recover; and all the time shells are shrieking and minie bullets whistling over and about me. The tongue becomes **parched**, there is no water to quench it; you cry, "Water! water!" and pray for night, that you can be carried off the field and to the hospital, and there the surgeons' care—maimed, crippled for life, perchance die. There are your **reflections**. Who can portray the horrors coming to the wounded?

The experiences of a man under fire differ **materially** between his first and subsequent engagements. Why? Because of discipline. "Familiarity with death **begets** contempt" is an old and true saying. With the new troops, they have not been called on to train or restrain their nerves. They are not only nervous, but they **blanch** at the thought of danger. They **want education**. What to them, on joining the service, was a terrible mental strain, is soon transformed into indifference. It is brought about by discipline.

What happened next . . .

Both Civil War armies experienced great difficulty in keeping unhappy or frightened soldiers from deserting (leaving the army before their term of service ended). Historians estimate that as many as two hundred thousand soldiers deserted from the Union Army during the war, while more than one hundred thousand troops deserted from the smaller Confederate military. Many of the Confederate soldiers who deserted did so very late in the war, when the Confederacy suffered numerous military defeats and its civilian population began to experience great hunger and poverty. "Hundreds of men are deserting nightly," wrote Confederate general Robert

Maintained: Continued.

Tourniquet: A device used to temporarily stop the flow of blood through a large artery in an arm or leg.

Same: A reference to the tourniquet.

Parched: Dry.

Reflections: Thoughts.

Materially: Significantly.

Begets: Produces.

Blanch: Turn pale.

Want education: Lack battlefield experience.

E. Lee (1807–1870) in early 1865. "I don't know what can be done to put a stop to it."

Did you know . . .

- During the course of the Civil War, several colorful phrases were used to describe actions and experiences on the field of battle. For example, both Northern and Southern troops referred to a soldier's first experience in combat as "seeing the elephant." Soldiers or military units who showed cowardice in battle, meanwhile, were accused of "showing the white feather."

- Many Civil War soldiers died of wounds that would not have been fatal if they could have received treatment in a modern medical facility. Back in the 1860s, however, infections and disease were much more widespread. Doctors of that period did not understand how diseases like malaria or typhoid fever spread. They did not even know that they should sterilize surgical instruments in order to prevent wounds from becoming infected.

The signal tower at the Union camp in Bermuda Hundred, Virginia. *(Courtesy of the Library of Congress.)*

For Further Reading

Commager, Henry Steele. *The Blue and the Gray: The Story of the Civil War as Told by Participants.* 2 vols. Indianapolis: Bobbs-Merrill, 1950.

Holsinger, Frank. *How Does One Feel Under Fire?* Leavenworth, KS, 1898.

McPherson, James M. *For Cause and Comrades: Why Men Fought in the Civil War.* New York: Oxford University Press, 1997.

Mitchell, Reid. *Civil War Soldiers.* New York: Oxford University Press, 1988.

Wiley, Bell Irvin. *The Life of Billy Yank: The Common Soldier of the Union.* Indianapolis: Bobbs-Merrill, 1952. Reprint, Garden City, NY: Doubleday, 1971.

Wiley, Bell Irvin. *The Life of Johnny Reb: The Common Soldier of the Confederacy.* Indianapolis: Bobbs-Merrill, 1943. Reprint, Baton Rouge: Louisiana State University Press, 1978.

William Willis Blackford

Excerpt from War Years with Jeb Stuart
Written in 1862; first published in 1945

A Confederate officer describes a daring cavalry raid

Both the Union and the Confederate militaries organized their armies into three major combat units. The largest and most important of these units was the infantry. The infantry consisted of soldiers who were trained to fight on foot. Most men who fought in the Civil War fit under this category. The Union's larger population and its superior ability to produce rifles, boots, and other gear used by infantry soldiers gave it a big advantage over the Confederate infantry during the war.

A second major arm of the Union and Confederate militaries was artillery. Artillery units consisted of soldiers who were trained to use cannons and other big guns. Since Northern cities had a far greater capacity to manufacture and transport cannons and ammunition than did cities in the South, the Union held a considerable edge in this important area of the war as well.

The third major combat unit of the two armies was cavalry. Cavalry units consisted of soldiers who were trained to scout and perform other duties on horseback. Unlike the other two organizational units, the Union army did not hold

"We were not half across when the bank we had left was swarming with the enemy who opened a galling fire upon us, the bullets splashing the water around us like a shower of rain."

The South Challenges the North in One of America's Most Famous Horse Races

Nearly forty years before Confederate and Union cavalrymen mounted horses to face each other in the Civil War, a less violent contest between riders from America's Southern and Northern regions captured the country's attention. This contest, which pitted a horse from the North named American Eclipse against a horse from the South named Sir Henry, was the first great horse racing event in American history.

By May 1823, when the race took place, many Americans had decided that the nation's finest horses were raised in the South. After all, wealthy Southern planters and businessmen had purchased many of the country's finest horses and transported them south, and most of the best horse breeding farms in America were located in the South.

Eager to prove the superiority of Southern horses once and for all, a wealthy Southern horse owner named Colonel William Ransom Johnson challenged the owner of American Eclipse, the finest horse in the North, to a race. American Eclipse's owner, Cornelius Van Ranst, accepted the challenge and told Johnson that he would race any horse in the entire South. Johnson selected one of his own horses, called Sir Henry, for the contest. The two men then agreed on a $20,000 bet on the race.

When news of the race was announced, the whole nation became caught up in the contest. Northerners expressed high hopes for American Eclipse. Southerners staked their regional pride on Sir Henry, which had won sixty-one of sixty-three

an advantage in this area. In fact, the Confederate cavalry was vastly superior to its Union counterpart, especially during the first two years of the Civil War.

Much of the Confederacy's advantage in cavalry could be traced to factors in Southern culture and society. Many Southern boys grew up in rural areas, where they were encouraged to develop their riding skills. After all, Southerners often had to travel great distances on horseback over land that featured rough or nonexistent roads in order to reach neighboring towns and plantations. In addition, many Southern families relied on hunting for food. Boys who grew up in such families learned to shoot rifles and find their way through woods at an early age. This combination of riding ability and marksmanship (the ability to shoot a gun well) races in its career. In many cases, people bet large amounts of money on the outcome. A wealthy Virginia planter, for example, agreed to give up five years' worth of cotton crops if Sir Henry lost. A Northern cotton mill owner, meanwhile, wagered three years of profits on an American Eclipse victory.

On the night before the race, more than fifty thousand people gathered at the Union Race Course on Long Island, New York, where the contest was scheduled to be held. Race fans filled every hotel within fifty miles of the course. Thousands of other people slept in wagons, camped in the woods, and waited on boats anchored offshore. The U.S. Congress even called a break so that its representatives could attend the big race.

The contest consisted of three races. Whichever horse won two out of the three races would be the victor. Southerners cheered wildly as Sir Henry won the first race. But American Eclipse won the second race so easily that even optimistic Southerners in the crowd wondered if their horse could win the contest. As it turned out, those fears proved accurate. Sir Henry galloped hard in the third and deciding race, but American Eclipse won easily to take the contest. As Northerners in the crowd celebrated, many Southerners expressed disappointment with the outcome. But although a few wild newspaper reports suggested that some Southerners committed suicide after the race, reliable witnesses say that fans of Sir Henry reacted to the defeat with grace and good humor.

made Southern men ideally suited for cavalry duty. Finally, Southern traditions led people to view cavalry soldiers as particularly dashing and romantic. In the South, "the legends of chivalry [having the qualities of honor, courage, and protecting women] were powerful," wrote Bruce Catton in *The Civil War*, "so that it seemed much more knightly and gallant to go off to war on horseback than in the infantry."

Northerners, on the other hand, were more likely to be raised in cities or on farms where horses were used for plowing fields and other labor rather than for transportation. Since Northern communities did not tend to emphasize the use of horses for riding, boys who grew up in Michigan, Ohio, New York, and other Northern states were less likely to be skilled horsemen. Northerners also did not pay as much attention to breeding horses for riding. In contrast, many Southern horse owners devoted a great deal of energy to developing fast, strong, and healthy mounts (horses). Since the South did not have the resources to provide its army with mounts, Confederate cavalry soldiers used their own horses during the conflict.

All of these factors enabled the South to establish complete cavalry dominance during the first two years of the war. In fact, when the Civil War began, many rebel cavalry units were made up of expert riders who roamed the countryside on high-quality mounts that they had ridden for years. By contrast, Northern cavalry units contained many inexperienced horsemen who were stuck riding inferior horses purchased by the army.

From 1861 to 1863, the Confederate Army took advantage of this superiority. Rebel cavalry units made full use of their ability to move quickly from one area to another. They became known for making swift strikes on Union railroads, supply centers, and other enemy positions. They also did a much better job of scouting enemy troop size and movements and preventing surprise attacks than did the North's cavalry. Finally, the generally superior marksmanship of Confederate cavalry made them more effective than their Union counterparts in battle.

By the midpoint of the war, Union military leaders viewed Confederate cavalry units as irritating pests that were nonetheless capable of delivering painful stings. Their scouting abilities made it much more difficult for Northern armies to surprise Confederate infantry and artillery forces. In addition, their habit of raiding Union supply lines forced Northern generals to use thousands of soldiers to guard railroads and telegraph lines. Union armies spent a great deal of their time and effort chasing Southern cavalry, but their attempts to capture or destroy the rebel riders were rarely successful. The soldiers in the Confederate cavalry "are splendid riders, first-rate shots, and utterly reckless," admitted Union general William T. Sherman (1820–1891). "They are the best cavalry in the world."

As the Civil War progressed, the glamorous reputation of cavalry service made it a favorite subject for newspaper coverage in both the South and the North. In fact, several

Confederate cavalry officers became famous for their daring raids and dramatic escapes. Notable Confederate cavalry leaders included Nathan Bedford Forrest (1821–1877), John Hunt Morgan (1825–1864), and Joseph Wheeler (1836–1906).

Another famous Southern cavalryman was Major General J. E. B. "Jeb" Stuart (1833 –1864). He commanded the cavalry forces in the Confederacy's Army of Northern Virginia, which was led by the legendary general Robert E. Lee. A smart and brave leader, Stuart led many successful raids on Union positions. In addition, reports from his cavalry scouts helped Lee make countless strategic decisions. Stuart was assisted on his missions by Lieutenant Colonel William Willis Blackford (1831–1905), who served on his staff from June 1861 to January 1864. In the following excerpt, Blackford tells about a daring cavalry raid Stuart led deep into Northern territory. This raid on Chambersburg, Pennsylvania, and other surrounding areas took place in October 1862, when the Confederate cavalry's dominance over the Union cavalry was at its height.

Confederate major general Jeb Stuart. (*Courtesy of the National Archives and Records Administration.*)

Things to remember while reading the excerpt from *War Years with Jeb Stuart:*

- As Blackford mentions, Stuart and other Confederate cavalry leaders made very good use of their troops' geographical knowledge. When they launched raids into enemy territory, they often used rebel soldiers who grew up in the area to guide them. The rebel cavalry also used their knowledge of Southern woodlands to frustrate invading Union troops. "The South was laced with obscure country roads not marked on any map," said James M. McPherson in *Ordeal by Fire.* "Only local knowledge could guide troops along these roads, many of which ran through thick woods that could shield the movement from the enemy but where a wrong turn could get a division hopelessly lost. . . . Numerous examples could . . . be cited of Union troops getting lost on similar roads because of inaccurate or nonexistent maps."

- Confederate cavalry raids were a constant nuisance to the North. The Southern attacks on railroad lines and other strategic Union positions forced Northern military leaders to use many of their men for guard duty. In addition, their successful raids of horses, food, and other supplies hurt the Union war effort and allowed the Confederate Army to send scarce supplies to other needy troops. Blackford estimated that in the raid on Chambersburg alone, Stuart's cavalrymen stole twelve hundred to fifteen hundred horses, freed hundreds of Confederate prisoners, and destroyed $250,000 worth of property belonging to Northerners.

Excerpt from War Years with Jeb Stuart

The force assembled at Darkesville and camped that night above Williamsport [Pennsylvania] *to cross* [the river] *at daylight on the 10th* [of October, 1862] *at McCoy's **ford**, and we captured the **picket** at that place. A large infantry force had just marched by, going westward. . . . The luck of not encountering this force at the **outset** was a source of congratulation for it might have caused such delay as to have made the trip **impracticable**. A signal station was also captured by surprise, and our movement thus concealed the longer. General Stuart had **capital** guides, soldiers of our army who knew every foot of the country and many of the people. Finding that the enemy had a large force at Hagerstown* [Maryland]*, the General determined to push northward to Chambersburg* [Pennsylvania]*. At Mercersburg* [Pennsylvania] *I found that a citizen of the place had a county map and of course called at the house for it, as these maps had every road laid down and would be of the greatest service to us. Only the females of the family appeared, who flatly refused to let me have the map, or to acknowledge that they had one; so I was obliged to dismount and push by the infuriated ladies, rather **rough specimens**, however, into the sitting room where I found the map*

Ford: A shallow place in a river where people can cross on foot or horseback.

Picket: Guard.

Outset: Beginning.

Impracticable: Impractical; not possible to accomplish.

Capital: Excellent.

Rough specimens: Vulgar or unrefined people.

*hanging on the wall. Angry women do not **show to advantage**, and the language and looks of these were fearful, as I coolly cut the map out of its rollers and put it in my **haversack**. . . .General Stuart determined to take nothing but horses, as cattle would have delayed our movements. That part of Pennsylvania was full of great, fat Conestoga horses of the Norman breed, most valuable animals for artillery purposes but wholly unfit for cavalry mounts. Everything was arranged, but no **plundering** was to take place until we had crossed the Maryland border. The men were wild with enthusiasm, and eagerly watched for the line across which the fun would begin. The middle division was arranged so that **parties** of half a dozen or a dozen under an officer were to dash out right and left to the farm houses and bring in the horses, which were then tied by their halters three together and led by a soldier riding alongside.*

*As good luck would have it the day was cloudy with occasional showers, and the thrifty Pennsylvania farmers were assembled in their huge barns **threshing** wheat. From every direction through the mist our **foraging** parties were guided to the spot by the droning hum of the threshers with which all these Pennsylvania barns are provided. For the fun of the thing I joined in several charges of this kind and in every case was rewarded by amusing scenes, to say nothing of the raids we made upon the well filled pantries at the houses. . . .*

*If the day had been fine and the people out in the fields, the news of our coming would no doubt have spread and not nearly so many horses would have been collected. A clean sweep of all on the place was generally made, but I remember that in one case I made an exception in a rather curious manner. . . . We had just taken an unusually nice looking lot of horses out of [a barn in Pennsylvania] when quite a **genteel** looking old lady came out and asked that we would let her keep her old driving horse, which she assured us was in the thirty-fifth year of his age. She said that she had owned him from a colt and knew him to be that old, and that he had long since done nothing but work in her buggy when she wanted to go anywhere, and that he would be of no use whatever to us. I asked her to point out the animal. . . . The moment I opened [the horse's] mouth I saw the old lady's account was true, his teeth were worn off level with the gums. This was an animal whose age was as seldom reached by his kind as that of a hundred and twenty-five years would be by a human being. Bowing to the old lady I returned her faithful and noble favorite, to her great delight.*

Show to advantage: Impress others.

Haversack: A bag for carrying supplies.

Plundering: Stealing of property.

Parties: Groups.

Threshing: Separating grain or seeds from straw.

Foraging: Searching for supplies.

Genteel: Elegant or refined.

During this long day's march everything indicated our coming to be unexpected, and not a shadow of opposition appeared. The truth was that their cavalry were afraid to meet us and gladly **availed themselves** of the **pretext** of not being able to find us. Up to this time the cavalry of the enemy had no more confidence in themselves than the country had in them, and whenever we got a chance at them, which was rarely, they came to grief.

[Stuart's army of cavalry then captured the small town of Chambersburg. After raiding the village's shops and farmhouses, Stuart decided to begin the journey back to Virginia. Since Stuart's cavalry was deep in enemy territory, he knew that the trip would be dangerous. But he believed that if his troops moved quickly and returned to Virginia by an unexpected route, he could avoid Union forces in the area.] *From a point about forty miles in rear of the enemy we were to march to a crossing of the Potomac [River] ten or fifteen miles below [Union general George McClellan's] position, passing within less than ten miles of his main **body**, so that for the greater part of the day we were going directly towards their camps. The march was the longest without a **halt** I have ever experienced. Starting from Chambersburg that morning we marched all that day, all that night and until four o'clock the next day before reaching Leesburg in Virginia; ninety miles with only one halt of half an hour to feed the horses the evening of the first day. It was only by riding captured horses and resting their own that the men could keep up, though I myself rode Magic [Blackford's horse] the whole time without change, fearing to [lose] her in case of a sudden attack. . . .*

*My place usually was with the **advanced guard** and I generally rode with the three **videttes** in front so as to report to the General at once anything we might encounter. Having my powerful **glasses**, I could see exactly the **character** of any body of men we came in sight of, and thus could tell whether those we saw at a distance were armed men or only country people and thus saving much delay in approaching them. General Stuart issued orders that no firearms were to be used in attack, nothing but the sabre alone until further orders. This was to prevent as much as possible the noise from giving **intelligence** of our position. . . . It seemed almost incredible that the enemy should not have discovered our position as the day wore on. Why their cavalry had not hung upon our rear and given intelligence of our route is **unaccountable**. The truth was, no doubt, that their cavalry was afraid of us, for up to that time our superiority in that arm of the **service** was unquestioned, and they seldom ventured*

Availed themselves: Took advantage.

Pretext: Excuse.

Body: Army.

Halt: Rest.

Advanced guard: Scouting party.

Videttes: Scouts stationed at the front of military movements.

Glasses: Binoculars.

Character: Identity.

Intelligence: Information about.

Unaccountable: Cannot be explained.

Service: Military.

Members of a Pennsylvania cavalry division gather in Brandy Station, Virginia. *(Courtesy of the Library of Congress.)*

within our reach, and whenever they did they **invariably** came to grief. But why a small party should not have followed us and given information can be attributed only to bad management, for they could have gotten the information in a friendly country without ever making an attack, by means of the citizens along the roads we passed. But so it was, as appears now from their official **dispatches**, that up to our reaching the river on our return, they had no exact intelligence of our movements. [At one point,] McClellan **inferred** we would attempt a crossing below him. He sent all of his cavalry to intercept us and some thirty miles from the river we passed within four miles of [Union general Alfred] Pleasanton and his large body of cavalry, but he knew not of our presence. . . .

[Stuart's cavalry marched all night through Pennsylvania and into Maryland.] *When day dawned on the morning of the 12th* [of October], *we entered Hayattstown, having made sixty-five miles from Chambersburg in twenty hours. It was this great speed which* **baffled** *the enemy who had by this time found out in a general man-*

Invariably: Always.

Dispatches: Messages.

Inferred: Concluded from available evidence.

Baffled: Confused.

ner that we were moving southward, and were crowding all their available troops towards our supposed route to intercept us. [Union generals George] *Stoneman and* [Alfred] *Pleasanton with their cavalry were in hot pursuit, infantry was strung along the river at every ford, and a large force was placed on trains of cars at Monocacy crossing ready to move to any point at which they might be needed. The most of these facts were discovered by Stuart from intercepted dispatches, and his **sagacity**, boldness and quickness were **taxed** to the utmost to meet the occasion. By changing horses frequently the artillery was enabled to keep up during the tremendous march we had made, but there was still twelve miles between us and the river, within which twelve miles the ruin of all our hopes might lie.*

*It was now that the services of Captain White as a guide became so valuable. This was where he had lived all his life and every by-road was well known to him. By marching down a road towards a lower ford to deceive the enemy and then suddenly turning down through a cart track in the woods White led the column to a ford that was little used and where we were little expected. While on the main road we overtook a scouting party of the enemy, the first troops we had met in the whole expedition, and charged them, putting them to **instant rout**. . . .*[Stuart's army then reached the river, where they fooled a Union regiment into retreating. Stuart then ordered his soldiers to cross the river as pursuing Yankee troops closed in.] *There was nothing to be done now but get the command across as quickly as possible. . . . A force was posted above and below* [the river crossing] *to oppose and hold in check the enemy who was advancing from both directions, while* [Confederate major John Pelham, who commanded Stuart's artillery forces] *pounded away with two **guns** first one side and then the other, with great spirit, on the heads of their **columns** in full view of us. It was of the utmost importance that the crossing should be **effected** without delay, and the captured horses were so famished for water that there was great danger of the narrow ford becoming choked with them while drinking; so General Stuart sent me to the ford with orders that no man should stop to water his horse while crossing the river. It was necessary to repeat the order to every company commander as he came by and to see that it was enforced, for sometimes the horses would stop in spite of everything and plunge their heads up to their eyes into the water to take deep **draughts** of what they so much needed.*

*Some guns were trotted across first to go into **battery** on the opposite bank to cover the crossing of the main body and the long*

Sagacity: Wisdom.

Taxed: Strained.

Instant rout: Total retreat.

Guns: Artillery or cannons.

Columns: Formation of soldiers moving in a unified group.

Effected: Performed or completed.

Draughts: Drinks.

Battery: Begin firing artillery shells.

The camp of a Pennsylvania cavalry troop. (*Courtesy of the Library of Congress.*)

*line of cavalry, and then the great horses which we had captured came rapidly past, led in couples. . . . The last files of the last division were entering the water when General Stuart rode down the bank to where I was and in a voice choked with emotion, and his eyes filling as he spoke, said, "Blackford, we are going to [lose] our rear guard." "How is that, General?" I asked in surprise. "Why," said he, "I have sent four **couriers** to [Confederate colonel M. C.] Butler to call him in, and he is not here, and you see the enemy is closing in upon us from above and below."*

[Blackford subsequently volunteered to go back and try to find Butler, even though Union troops were closing in quickly.] *The place where I expected to find Butler was passed, and on and on I went. One, two, and over three miles, until I gave up all hope of getting to him in time to save his **command**; but to find him I was determined, and kept on. At last at a sudden turn of the road I dashed right into the rear guard. . . . Going on to where Butler was I called him aside and explained the situation to him. In a moment we*

Couriers: Messengers.

Command: Troops under his command.

William Willis Blackford | 59

were in motion at a trot, but I leaned over and told Butler we must move faster or we would be cut off, that General Stuart said he must come in at a gallop. [Butler subsequently ordered his command into a full gallop, even though they were hauling a cannon.] *He was very reluctant to abandon the gun, and to our surprise and pleasure the horses held out and brought the gun in safely. . . . As we approached the ford Colonel Butler got everything ready for a charge if it should be necessary to cut our way through to the ford, and with drawn sabres we dashed into the field where the entrance to the ford was. There stood Pelham with his piece and there the enemy, just as I had left them, with an open gap between for us to pass through. In a moment we were at the ford and Pelham's gun rumbling along after us into the water.*

*We were not half across when the bank we had left was swarming with the enemy who opened a **galling** fire upon us, the bullets splashing the water around us like a shower of rain. But the [Confederate] guns from the Virginia side immediately opened on them and **mitigated** their fire considerably, and we soon crossed and stood once more on Virginia soil. The march was continued a few miles farther to Leesburg, where we encamped that afternoon as weary a **set** as ever dismounted.*

What happened next . . .

The Confederate cavalry continued to dominate Union cavalry units through the beginning of 1863. Gradually, however, the performance of Northern cavalrymen improved. Historians trace this change to several factors. First, the long months of hard training that Union cavalry endured finally began to pay off, as soldiers learned to become good riders. Union cavalry forces also benefitted from improved military leadership. During the first two years of the war, cavalry were often used poorly by the Union Army. But when soldiers like General Ulysses S. Grant (1822–1885) and General William T. Sherman took control of the Northern war effort, they used Union cavalry much more effectively. Finally, the Union Army began outfitting several cavalry units with seven-shot repeating rifles (rifles that could be shot seven times before a soldier had to stop shooting to reload) that were better than the guns used by rebel soldiers. These repeating rifles greatly increased the effectiveness of Union cavalrymen in combat.

Union cavalry forces also benefitted from growing problems within some Confederate cavalry units. In 1863 and 1864, rebel cavalry units experienced shortages of both soldiers and horses. Blackford admitted that from mid-1863 onward, "the difficulty of getting remounts [new horses] acted disastrously upon the strength of our cavalry arm, not only in diminishing the numbers but in impairing the spirit of the men. . . . The most dashing trooper was the one whose horse was the most apt to be shot, and when this man was unable to remount himself he had to go to the infantry service, and was lost to the cavalry. Such a penalty for gallantry was terribly demoralizing."

As the Union cavalry gained experience and the Confederate cavalry struggled with shortages of men and horses, the long-time Southern dominance in this area came to an end. One clear indication of the South's diminishing cavalry advantage came in June 1863, when a big battle between Union and Confederate cavalry forces at Brandy Station, Virginia, ended in a draw. By late 1863, Blackford was forced to acknowledge that "the cavalry of the enemy were steadily improving and it was all we could do sometimes to manage them." Only the skilled leadership of Southern cavalry leaders like Jeb Stuart enabled the Confederacy to match the Federal (Union) cavalry performance during the last two years of the war.

Stuart continued to command the cavalry arm of the Confederate Army of Northern Virginia until May 11, 1864, when he was mortally wounded in a battle with Union cavalry forces led by General Philip Sheridan (1831–1888) outside of Richmond, Virginia. His death one day later was a tremendous blow to the South. After Stuart died, Confederate general Robert E. Lee admitted that "I can scarcely think of him without weeping." Lieutenant Colonel William Willis Blackford, meanwhile, served in the Confederate Army until the war ended. After the war, he worked as a railroad engineer and designer and as superintendent of the Virginia Polytechnic Institute campus. He died in 1905.

Did you know . . .

- Stuart's dramatic raid of Chambersburg made him famous throughout America. In fact, the raid even captured the imagination of foreign newspapers. In October 1862, for example, the London *Times* declared that "anything more daring, more gallant, and more successful than the foray [raid] of General Stuart . . . over the border of Maryland and Pennsylvania, has never been recorded."

- Cavalrymen on both sides often became very emotionally attached to their horses. This was especially true in the case of Confederate soldiers, who often used horses that they had been riding for years. One example of this loyalty to individual horses can be seen in Blackford's narrative. As Stuart's cavalry pushes southward in order to avoid pursuing Union troops, Blackford admits that he should ride one of the captured horses so that his horse Magic can rest a little. But he continues to ride Magic because he fears that he might lose her if their army comes under attack.

- During the opening months of the Civil War, many Northern communities became convinced that the Confederacy had formed a deadly "Black Horse Cavalry." This cavalry did not really exist, but Northern newspapers and magazines warned their readers about it all the time during the first year of the war. Fears about this imaginary cavalry actually ended up having an impact on the Civil War's first major battle, the First Battle of Bull Run (July 1861). When the Confederate Army gained an advantage in this clash in northern Virginia, Union military leaders decided to retreat. But this organized retreat turned into a panicked flight when frightened Northern civilians who had gone to watch the battle heard a rumor that the Black Horse Cavalry would soon swoop down and kill them all.

- Confederate and Union cavalries made many valuable contributions to the war effort for their respective sides. Even so, many soldiers who served in infantry or artillery units resented the extra praise and admiration that cavalrymen received from newspaper editors and ordinary citizens. Noting that cavalrymen engaged in fewer major battles than infantry and artillery units, they also felt that cavalry soldiers did not face the same dangers as ordinary soldiers. These feelings sometimes led bitter infantry soldiers to ask, "Who ever saw a dead cavalryman?"

For Further Reading

Blackford, William Willis. *War Years with Jeb Stuart.* New York: Scribner, 1945. Reprint, Baton Rouge: Louisiana State University Press, 1993.

Carter, Samuel. *The Last Cavaliers: Confederate and Union Cavalry in the Civil War.* New York: St. Martin's Press, 1980.

Longacre, Edward C. *Mounted Raids of the Civil War.* South Brunswick, NJ: A. S. Barnes, 1975. Reprint, Lincoln: University of Nebraska Press, 1994.

Thomas, Emory M. *Bold Dragoon: The Life of J. E. B. Stuart.* New York: Harper & Row, 1986. Reprint, Norman: University of Oklahoma Press, 1999.

Abraham Lincoln

The Emancipation Proclamation
Issued January 1, 1863

The president frees the slaves

B y the time President Abraham Lincoln (1809–1865) issued his final Emancipation Proclamation on January 1, 1863, he had been considering the idea of freeing the slaves for some time. Lincoln had believed that slavery was wrong when he was elected president in 1860. He felt that black people were entitled to the same legal rights as white people. When the Civil War began in 1861, he knew that freeing the slaves would hurt the Confederate war effort and aid the Union. But he still wanted to proceed carefully, because he knew that emancipation (the act of freeing people from slavery or oppression) had many opponents, even in the North. The president was particularly concerned about the reaction of the four slave-holding "border" states that had remained loyal to the Union—Maryland, Delaware, Missouri, and Kentucky. He worried that if he suddenly outlawed slavery, these states would leave the Union and join the Confederacy.

The U.S. Congress took the first step toward freeing the slaves in August 1861. At that time, it passed a law that allowed the Union Army to seize enemy property that was used in the war effort. Slaves were considered property in the South

> "I do order and declare that all persons held as slaves within said designated States and parts of States are, and henceforward shall be, free. . . ."

and were often used as laborers in Confederate Army camps. In effect, the Confiscation Act enabled Union troops to take any slaves they found away from their owners. Such slaves became known as "contrabands." Another law passed in March 1862 forbade Union Army officers from returning fugitive slaves to their owners in the South. In July 1862, Congress passed an even stronger Confiscation Act that granted freedom to any slaves who came under the control of Union troops. They also gave the president power to use these freed slaves as laborers or even soldiers in the Union Army.

Also in July 1862, President Lincoln read the first draft of his Emancipation Proclamation to his cabinet (a group of trusted advisors who supervised various government departments). His secretary of state, William H. Seward (1801–1872), suggested that he wait to issue it until the Union Army achieved a victory on the battlefield. Seward argued that if the president issued his proclamation at a time when the Union's chances of winning the Civil War seemed slim, it would be dismissed as a desperate attempt to avoid defeat. But if he waited until events went in the Union's favor, then the proclamation would seem more like a statement of moral principle. The proclamation would make it clear that the North was fighting not only to restore the Union, but also on behalf of basic American values of freedom and liberty for all men and women.

The Union Army managed to win a brutal battle at Antietam in Maryland in September 1862. Lincoln took this opportunity to issue a preliminary Emancipation Proclamation on September 22. This document warned the Confederate states that the president planned to free the slaves as of January 1, 1863, unless those states voluntarily rejoined the Union before that time. Since Lincoln was issuing the Emancipation Proclamation as a war measure, it would only apply to enemy territory—those states that were in rebellion against the United States. It would not apply to areas in the South that had been captured and occupied by Union troops, or to the slave-holding border states that were still part of the Union. This meant that 830,000 black men and women would remain slaves out of a total of 4 million slaves in the South.

Many people found it strange that Lincoln granted freedom to the slaves in Confederate states. Since those states had

seceded from (left) the United States at the beginning of the Civil War, the American government had no power to enforce such an order there. The slaves might be emancipated according to a piece of paper, but in reality they would not be free until Union troops arrived. Some Northern abolitionists were disappointed that the Emancipation Proclamation would not apply to the border states or to occupied areas. As a writer for the *London Spectator* noted, the proclamation did not say "that a human being cannot justly own another, but that he cannot own him unless he is loyal to the United States." Some people doubted whether the president's proclamation was even legal. Lincoln issued the order under the broad powers that the Constitution gives the president in times of war as commander-in-chief of the U.S. Army. But the Constitution allowed slavery, and only Congress holds the power to propose changes to the Constitution.

Despite these criticisms, Lincoln issued his final Emancipation Proclamation on January 1, 1863. It was "one

President Abraham Lincoln discusses the first draft of the Emancipation Proclamation with his cabinet. *(Courtesy of the Library of Congress.)*

of the strangest and most important state papers ever issued by an American President," according to Bruce Catton in *The Civil War.*

Things to remember while reading Abraham Lincoln's Emancipation Proclamation:

- President Lincoln's proclamation did not free all the slaves in the United States. In fact, it only freed the slaves in the Confederate states that had left the Union. It did not apply to the four slave-holding border states that remained part of the Union. It also did not apply to the areas of Southern states that were under control of the Union Army at the time it was issued. Lincoln outlines which states he means in the second paragraph of the document. The exceptions he mentions are areas that were loyal to the Union or were under Union control. He explains that these areas will be "left precisely as if this proclamation were not issued," meaning that slavery would continue to exist there, at least "for the present."

- Upon hearing about the Emancipation Proclamation, some Southerners accused the president of trying to help the Union's war effort by causing slave uprisings across the Confederacy. Lincoln addresses this issue in the fourth paragraph of the document. He expressly asks freed slaves not to engage in violence, unless they are forced to defend themselves.

- In the fifth paragraph of the document, Lincoln declares his intention to use freed slaves in the Union Army. This was a relatively new idea at the time the Emancipation Proclamation was issued. Discrimination had prevented black men from serving in the Union Army until late 1862.

Abraham Lincoln's Emancipation Proclamation

*I, Abraham Lincoln, President of the United States, by virtue of the power in me **vested** as Commander-in-Chief of the Army and*

Vested: Guaranteed as a legal right or privilege.

Navy of the United States in time of actual armed **rebellion** against the authority and government of the United States, and as a fit and necessary war measure for **suppressing** said rebellion, do, on this 1st day of January, A.D. 1863, and in accordance with my purpose so to do, publicly proclaimed for the full period of one hundred days from the first day above mentioned, order and designate as the States and parts of States wherein the people thereof, respectively, are this day in rebellion against the United States the following, to wit:

Arkansas, Texas, Louisiana (except the **parishes** of St. Bernard, Plaquemines, Jefferson, St. John, St. Charles, St. James, Ascension, Assumption, Terrebonne, Lafourche, St. Mary, St. Martin, and Orleans, including the city of New Orleans), Mississippi, Alabama, Florida, Georgia, South Carolina, North Carolina, and Virginia (except for the forty-eight counties designated as West Virginia, and also the counties of Berkeley, Accomac, Northhampton, Elizabeth City, York, Princess Anne, and Norfolk, including the cities of Norfolk and Portsmouth), and which excepted parts are for the present left precisely as if this **proclamation** were not issued.

And by virtue of the power and for the purpose aforesaid, I do order and declare that all persons held as slaves within said designated States and parts of States are, and henceforward shall be, free; and that the Executive Government of the United States, including the military and naval authorities thereof, will recognize and maintain the freedom of said persons.

And I hereby **enjoin** upon the people so declared to be free to **abstain** from all violence, unless in necessary self-defense; and I recommend to them that, in all cases when allowed, they labor faithfully for reasonable wages.

And I further declare and make known that such persons of suitable condition will be received into the armed service of the United States to **garrison** forts, positions, stations, and other places, and to man vessels of all sorts in said service.

And upon this act, sincerely believed to be an act of justice, **warranted** by the Constitution upon military necessity, I invoke the considerate judgment of mankind and the gracious favor of Almighty God.

Rebellion: Resistance or defiance of an established government.

Suppressing: Subduing or putting down by force.

Parishes: Divisions of the state of Louisiana that are the equivalent of counties in other states.

Proclamation: An official public announcement.

Enjoin: Direct or command.

Abstain: Prevent oneself from taking an action.

Garrison: To occupy with troops.

Warranted: Authorized or supported.

What happened next . . .

Reactions to Lincoln's announcement were divided along predictable lines in the South. White Southerners criticized the Emancipation Proclamation, while slaves and free blacks in the South supported it. The Confederate government said that Lincoln had no authority to make such a statement and encouraged people to disregard it. Many whites claimed that the president issued the document in hopes of creating widespread slave rebellions across the South.

As slaves in the South heard about the Emancipation Proclamation, they began to recognize what the Civil War meant for their future. If the North won, slavery would be abolished (completely eliminated) throughout the land. As a result, some slaves began to rebel against their masters and to help the Union cause. Some simply refused to work, while others started fires to destroy property belonging to whites. Thousands of slaves decided to flee the South for freedom in the North. This movement deprived the Confederacy of a valuable labor force and helped increase the size of Union forces. Although most slaves were thrilled to learn that they were free, some also recognized that freedom brought uncertainty and new responsibilities. Since many slaves had not received basic education and were not trained in any special skills, they were concerned about how they would make a living and take care of their families.

In the North, early reactions to the Emancipation Proclamation were mixed. Abolitionists and free blacks were thrilled by the news. They recognized the president's reasons for proceeding cautiously, and they knew that the document was still a revolutionary one even if it did not immediately free all of the nation's slaves. After all, the proclamation said that any slaves who were freed during the war would remain "forever free." It also promised that the U.S. government would "recognize and maintain" their freedom. So they felt that the document would have some positive effects regardless of the final outcome of the war. At the same time, some Northerners opposed the idea of freeing the slaves. Some working-class whites worried that former slaves would come to the North and take their jobs. Other Northerners felt that emancipation would prolong the war and cost more lives.

Reaction was mixed among soldiers in the Union Army as well. Many Northern soldiers did not feel strongly about outlawing slavery prior to the war. Instead, they fought in order to preserve the Union. Other soldiers, particularly those who came from slave-holding border states, actually supported slavery. By the middle of 1863, however, most Union soldiers had accepted the idea of emancipation. For one thing, they recognized that freeing the slaves hurt the Confederate war effort by taking away valuable property as "contraband of war." For another thing, black soldiers began contributing to Union victories in battle. As white soldiers saw the courage of their black counterparts, many came to believe that emancipation would help the Union win the war.

As Northern support for emancipation increased in the months following Lincoln's announcement, it changed the way many people viewed the Civil War. The Emancipation Proclamation made it clear that the North was fighting for a broader cause than simply restoring the Union. They were also fighting for the cause of human freedom. "The Emancipation Proclamation announced a new war aim," James M. McPherson wrote in *Ordeal by Fire: The Civil War and Reconstruction*. "The Union army became officially an army of liberation. The North was now fighting to create a new Union, not to restore the old one."

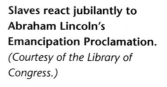

Slaves react jubilantly to Abraham Lincoln's Emancipation Proclamation. *(Courtesy of the Library of Congress.)*

Did you know . . .

- The process of ending slavery that began with the Emancipation Proclamation was completed with the Thirteenth Amendment to the U.S. Constitution. This amendment, which permanently outlawed slavery in the

United States, was passed by Congress in January 1865 and ratified (approved) by the states in the fall of that year.

- Martin Luther King, Jr.—one of the leaders of the American civil rights movement of the 1960s—made his famous "I Have a Dream" speech on January 1, 1963, at a ceremony to honor the one hundredth anniversary of the Emancipation Proclamation. King acknowledged that black people still faced discrimination in American society, but expressed his hope that they would soon achieve true equality. At one point in the speech, King said: "I have a dream that one day, on the red hills of Georgia, sons of former slaves and sons of former slaveowners will be able to sit down together at the table of brotherhood."

For Further Reading

Berlin, Ira. *Freedom: A Documentary History of Emancipation.* New York: Cambridge University Press, 1985.

Cox, LaWanda. *Lincoln and Black Freedom: A Study in Presidential Leadership.* Columbia: University of South Carolina Press, 1981.

Franklin, John Hope. *The Emancipation Proclamation.* Garden City, NY: Doubleday, 1963. Reprint, Wheeling, IL: Harlan Davidson, 1995.

McPherson, James M. *The Struggle for Equality: Abolitionists and the Negro in the Civil War and Reconstruction.* Princeton, NJ: Princeton University Press, 1964, 1995.

Trefousse, Hans L. *Lincoln's Decision for Emancipation.* Philadelphia: Lippincott, 1975.

Wood, Forrest G. *Black Scare: The Racist Response to Emancipation and Reconstruction.* Berkeley: University of California Press, 1968.

Richard Cordley

Account of William C. Quantrill's 1863 Raid on Lawrence, Kansas
First published separately in 1863, 1895, and 1903

A survivor details a bloody massacre of civilians

During the American Civil War, organized bands of Confederate fighters known as guerrillas were an important factor in the struggle for control of Missouri, Kansas, western Virginia, and other regions in question. These guerrillas—also known in the North as bushwhackers and in the South as rangers—launched repeated raids against Union supply lines, outposts, and patrols on behalf of the Confederacy. Bands of pro-Union guerrillas known as "jayhawkers" also formed in some of these areas, but they were smaller in number and size, and they did not have nearly the same impact as their Confederate counterparts.

Bands of Confederate guerrillas formed almost as soon as the war began. These early units consisted primarily of farmers and other local men who joined together in order to fight or harass Union forces operating in the region where they lived. The guerrilla companies had loose ties to the Confederate Army. The Confederate War Department encouraged and provided aid to guerrilla leaders from the war's outset. In April 1862, the Confederate Congress authorized the formation of ranger companies that were supposed to operate

> "[The guerrillas'] horses scarcely seemed to touch the ground, and the riders sat upon them with bodies erect and arms perfectly free with revolvers on full cock, shooting at every house and man they passed, and yelling like demons at every bound."

under the direction of the South's military commanders. In many cases, though, these guerrilla companies functioned with little supervision.

As Confederate guerrilla bands formed in Missouri, Arkansas, and other regions impacted by the war, ranger leaders found that it was easy to recruit members. Many Southerners joined the guerrilla groups because it gave them an opportunity to defend their home counties or states without leaving their farms or families. Other men were attracted to the guerrilla bands because most of them did not require members to obey many military rules and regulations. Still others joined guerrilla groups because of their glamorous wartime image in the South. Finally, outlaws were attracted to the bands because it gave them opportunities to enrich themselves by stealing from guerrilla targets.

Bands of Confederate guerrillas operated in regions that tended to be friendly to their cause. Pro-Confederacy civilians (people who are not part of the army, including women and children) often helped the guerrillas by providing food, clothing, weapons, and information about Union troop movements. Union attempts to stop the "bushwhackers" sometimes included harsh treatment of people and villages suspected of helping the guerrillas. As a result, Union efforts to stamp out the bushwhackers often had the unintended effect of *increasing* support for the Confederate guerrillas in rural towns and country farmhouses.

As the war progressed, a number of the Confederate guerrilla bands proved to be very effective in harassing the North's armies and supply lines. Daring raids on Union wagon trains, camps, and towns disrupted many Federal campaigns and forced Union commanders to divert (turn aside) large numbers of troops to capture the rangers. In some states, like Missouri, the warfare between Confederate ranger companies and Union forces ordered to stop them became extremely vicious. Innocent civilians sometimes got caught in the struggle between the two factions.

The most feared and respected of the Confederate guerrilla commanders was undoubtedly John Singleton Mosby (1833–1916). His band, known as Mosby's Rangers, struck repeatedly against Union forces throughout northern Virginia from 1863 through 1865. Led by their brilliant and courageous leader, Mosby's Rangers stole Union supplies, destroyed Union communication lines, and attacked Union patrols with deadly effectiveness. After each strike, Mosby's Rangers disappeared into the countryside, escaping from their frustrated pursuers. Mosby and his men were so effective in their campaigns against Federal troops that the northern Virginia region acquired the nickname of "Mosby's Confederacy."

But Mosby's band of guerrillas was unusual in several respects. The unit benefitted not only from Mosby's strategic brilliance, but also from his insistence on discipline. Unlike other bands of bushwhackers, Mosby's men wore Confederate uniforms and behaved much more like a regular army unit. By contrast, many other guerrilla groups became primarily known for drunkenness and senseless violence as the war progressed.

By 1863, the growing lawlessness of some guerrilla bands led a number of Southern leaders to question their value to the Confederate cause. These critics argued that the guerrilla bands drained men away from the shrinking Confederate Army. They also claimed that growing reports of vicious guerrilla attacks on pro-Union civilians and murders of surrendering soldiers were increasing Northern determination to punish the South. Finally, they claimed that some guerrilla actions were so immoral (ethically wrong or evil) that they were making the entire Confederacy look bad.

One of the most notorious of the Confederate guerrilla outfits was the band led by William C. Quantrill (1837–1865). Before the war, Quantrill had been a Kansas out-

Confederate guerrilla commander John Singleton Mosby. *(Courtesy of the Library of Congress.)*

William Clarke Quantrill (1837–1865)

A native of Dover, Ohio, William Quantrill first arrived in Kansas Territory in March 1857. For the next few years, he supported himself by working as a farmer, schoolteacher, and prospector. In 1860, however, he joined a small band of outlaws and became involved in kidnapping, horse theft, and other crimes. Quantrill—who called himself Charley Hart during this period of his life—also became strongly sympathetic to Southern complaints about Northern bullying and arrogance during this time. These feelings led him to side with the South when the American Civil War broke out in April 1861.

Quantrill served in the regular Confederate Army in the first months of the Civil War. In the fall, however, he emerged as the leader of a group of Missourians that had formed in order to stop attacks by "jayhawkers" (pro-Union guerrillas operating in Missouri and Kansas). Quantrill's band soon developed into a deadly guerrilla force that waged skillful attacks on Union patrols and disrupted various Union operations.

In August 1862, Quantrill's raiders led a successful attack on Independence, Missouri. This victory placed the town in Confederate hands and made Quantrill's reputation as one of the Confederacy's most feared guerrilla leaders. In 1863 Quantrill's company—which included a number of ruthless killers—became known for its cruelty and violence. In August 1863, they slaughtered more than 150 people in an attack on Lawrence, Kansas. Several weeks later, Quantrill and his band of over three hundred men killed almost one hundred inexperienced Union recruits—many of them unarmed—in a slaughter known as the Baxter Springs Massacre.

law named Charley Hart. After the Civil War began, he changed his name and organized a guerrilla group in Missouri. On some occasions, Quantrill's raiders provided a great deal of help to the Confederate cause. His fierce rangers, many of whom were superb marksmen and riders, conducted numerous successful raids on Union positions. They also led a successful rebel drive to run Union troops out of Independence, Missouri, in August 1862.

But Quantrill's band of bushwhackers also attracted large numbers of thieves and deserters (men who left the army illegally before their term of service ended) from the

In 1864, Quantrill lost control of his raiders after a power struggle with George Todd. He then organized a smaller group of bushwhackers in Kentucky. Quantrill continued leading violent raids until May 1865, when he was shot by Federal soldiers. He died of his wounds a month later, on June 6, 1865.

Quantrill was buried in an unmarked grave in Louisville, Kentucky. In 1887, however, a boyhood friend of Quantrill's named William Walter Scott arranged to have his remains unearthed. Scott took Quantrill's skull and several other bones and returned to Dover, Ohio. Quantrill's mother wanted to bury her son's remains in the Dover cemetery. At first, the community's political leaders refused to grant permission for the burial. They finally allowed it when Quantrill's mother agreed to leave the burial plot unmarked.

But without the knowledge of Mrs. Quantrill, Scott kept Quantrill's skull and a number of other bones for himself. He donated most of these bones to the Kansas State Historical Society in the 1890s. Quantrill's skull, meanwhile, passed through a number of hands after Scott's death in 1902. The skull was even used in fraternity initiation ceremonies during the 1920s and 1930s. It eventually came to belong to the Dover Historical Society, which displayed it in a local museum for many years. The bones held by the Kansas State Historical Society were finally buried on October 24, 1992, in the Confederate Cemetery at Higginsville, Missouri, in a ceremony that was attended by about six hundred people. Quantrill's skull was buried in Dover six days later.

regular Confederate Army. Aided by murderous lieutenants like George Todd and "Bloody Bill" Anderson, Quantrill built a renegade (outlaw) force that became known for its ruthlessness and thieving ways. In fact, by 1863 Quantrill's band included "some of the most psychopathic killers in American history," wrote historian James M. McPherson in *Battle Cry of Freedom.* Not all of Quantrill's men were cold-blooded murderers. Some members of his band remained primarily interested in striking against the Union forces that were invading their homeland. As the Civil War progressed, however, Quantrill and many of his followers seemed more interested in robbing people for their own personal gain and "killing for the sake of killing," as one Union officer said.

In mid-1863, Quantrill made plans to attack Lawrence, Kansas. Lawrence had long been a center of pro-Union and abolitionist (a person who fought to end slavery and oppression) activity. The city served as a major stopping point on the Underground Railroad (a secret organization devoted to helping slaves escape from the South and gain freedom in the North) and an important recruiting center for Union troops. It also was home to a large antislavery population that had fought hard to prevent supporters of slavery from legalizing the practice in Kansas. All of these factors made Lawrence an unpopular city among Confederates. But Quantrill also had a personal reason for targeting the city for violence. Before the war even started, he had been forced to flee from the Lawrence area after a warrant was issued for his arrest for theft and other crimes.

On the morning of August 21, 1863, Quantrill and a force of approximately 450 raiders charged into Lawrence. Normally, Lawrence was fairly well protected by Union forces. But poor military decisions had made the city practically defenseless, and Quantrill's raiders encountered little resistance from the unprepared townspeople. Over the next several hours, Quantrill and his men roamed through the town, murdering nearly every man or male youth whom they found. Historians estimate that between 150 and 200 men—young and old—were murdered by Quantrill's band. Many of these victims were shot in front of their wives and children. Quantrill's raiders also set fire to the community's business district and burned more than one hundred homes to the ground. After terrorizing the men, women, and children of Lawrence for several hours, Quantrill's bushwhackers finally rode out of town, their saddle bags bulging with loot stolen from ransacked homes and shops. They left behind a ruined city and dozens of stunned and grieving families.

One survivor of the attack—a minister named Richard Cordley—wrote three different accounts of the massacre at Lawrence, Kansas. The first of these accounts, "The Lawrence Massacre," was published in *The Congregational Record* in September and October of 1863. Years later, Cordley wrote two books *(A History of Lawrence, Kansas,* Lawrence Journal Press,

1895; and *Pioneer Days in Kansas,* Pilgrim Press, 1903) in which he offered additional details on Quantrill's bloody raid. In 1996, historian Edward E. Leslie blended excerpts from all three accounts in his book *The Devil Knows How to Ride: The True Story of William Clarke Quantrill and His Confederate Raiders.* The following excerpt is taken from Leslie's book.

Things to remember while reading Richard Cordley's account of the massacre at Lawrence, Kansas:

- The destruction in Lawrence would probably have been even worse were it not for the courage of the women in the town. "The ladies were wonderfully brave and efficient that morning," Cordley noted. "Some of them, by their shrewdness and suavity [gracious social manner], turned raiders from their purpose when they came to their houses. Sometimes they outwitted them, and at other times they boldly confronted and resisted them. In scores of cases they put the fires out as soon as those who kindled them left the house. In some cases they defiantly followed the raiders around, and extinguished the flames as they were kindled." Even the murderous Quantrill was impressed with their courage. After the massacre, he described the women of Lawrence as "brave and plucky."

- Some Confederate guerrilla units only targeted Union troops or people whom they knew were aiding the Federal cause. Mosby's Rangers, for example, stole horses, guns, food, and other supplies during their missions, but they did so in order to hurt the enemy rather than to enrich themselves. But as Cordley explains, Quantrill's guerrillas and many other bands of bushwhackers used the war as an excuse to murder and steal for personal gain.

- Many of the men who were shot by Quantrill's raiders were unarmed. Several others were burned to death when their homes and shops were set on fire with them inside. Quantrill actively encouraged this horrible violence. He told his men to "kill every man big enough to carry a gun."

Cordley's Account
of Quantrill's Raid on Lawrence

*The horsemanship of the guerrillas was perfect. They rode with that ease and **abandon** which are acquired only by a life spent in the saddle **amid** desperate scenes. Their horses scarcely seemed to touch the ground, and the riders sat upon them with bodies erect and arms perfectly free with revolvers on full cock, shooting at every house and man they passed, and yelling like demons at every bound. On each side of this stream of fire . . . were men falling dead and wounded, and women and children, running and screaming— some trying to escape from danger and some rushing to the side of their murdered friends. . . .*

[Cordley escaped from the town with his wife and child. After Quantrill's raiders left, Cordley returned to see how badly Lawrence had been damaged.] *The buildings on Massachusetts street were all burned except one, and that had been **ransacked** and robbed, and two boys lay dead upon the floor. The fires were still glowing in the cellars. The brick and stone walls were still standing bare and blackened. The cellars between looked like great caverns with furnaces glowing in the depths. The dead lay all along the street, some of them so **charred** that they could not be recognized, and could scarcely be taken up. Here and there among the embers could be seen the bones of those who had perished in the buildings and been **consumed** where they fell. . . . The sickening odor of burning flesh was **oppressive**. . . . Around one corner lay seventeen bodies. Back of a livery stable on Henry street lay five bodies piled in a heap. The **undermost** man of these was alive, and had lain under the dead for four hours, and so saved himself from a fatal shot. He was severely wounded but recovered. Going over the town [I] saw the dead everywhere, on the sidewalks, in the streets, among the weeds in the gardens, and in the few remaining homes. The women were going about carrying water to the wounded, and covering the dead with sheets. To protect the wounded from the burning sun, they sometimes spread an umbrella over them, and sometimes made a **canopy** with a sheet or a shawl. Now and then [I] came across a group, a mother and her children watching their dead besides the ashes of their home. A little later there could be seen a*

Abandon: Fearlessness.

Amid: Surrounded by; in the middle of.

Ransacked: Searched through.

Charred: Scorched or burned.

Consumed: Destroyed.

Oppressive: Overwhelming.

Undermost: Lowest.

Canopy: A high structure or covering held above a person or place for protection against sun or rain.

woman sitting among the ashes of a building holding in her hands a blackened skull, fondling it and kissing it, and crying **piteously** over it. It was the skull of her husband, who was burned with the building. But there was not much weeping and not much **wailing**. It was too deep and serious for tears or **lamentations**. All addressed themselves to the sad work that had to be done.

No one realized the extent of the disaster until it was over. Every man was so isolated by the presence of the raiders in every part of the town, that each knew only what he saw. . . . Besides the buildings on the business street, about one hundred houses had been burned, and probably as many more had been set on fire and saved by the heroic **exertions** of the women. Most of the houses not burned were robbed. . . . So many had been killed that every man we met on the street seemed to come from the dead. The first **salutation** was: "Why, are you alive?" The embers were still red, the fires were still burning, as we began to gather the dead and wounded from among the ruins. . . .

[The survivors then hurried to build coffins in order to bury their loved ones.] Many carpenters were killed, and most of the living had lost their tools. But they **rallied** nobly, and worked night and day, making pine and walnut boxes, fastening them together with the burnt nails gathered from the ruins of the stores. It sounded harsh to the ears of friends to have the lid nailed over the bodies of their loved ones; but it was the best that could be done.

What happened next . . .

The slaughter in Lawrence, Kansas, shocked and outraged communities all across the North. "Quantrill's massacre at Lawrence is almost enough to curdle the blood with horror," stated the *New York Times*. "We find it impossible to believe that men who have ever borne the name of Americans can have been transformed into such fiends [people who are inhumanely cruel]." In the aftermath of the attack, most Northerners viewed all Confederate guerrillas as depraved (morally corrupt) outlaws with no regard for human life. The Union Army, meanwhile, ordered the entire civilian population of four western Missouri counties to leave their homes. This strategy aimed to take away sources of aid for the guer-

Piteously: Pathetically or sadly.

Wailing: Long, intense crying.

Lamentations: Cries of sadness or mourning.

Exertions: Strenuous actions or efforts.

Salutation: Greeting.

Rallied: Joined together to work for a common cause.

rillas, but mostly it just caused misery for uprooted families—both pro-Union and pro-Confederacy—who were forced to build new lives for themselves elsewhere.

The massacre at Lawrence also horrified many Southerners. Confederate general Henry E. McCulloch was Quantrill's military superior, but he expressed uncertainty about his authority over Quantrill and horror over the raid on Lawrence. "I do not know what his military status is," McCulloch wrote. "I do not know as much about his mode of warfare as others seem to know; but, from all I can learn, it is but little, if at all, removed from that of the wildest savage. . . . We cannot, as a Christian people, sanction [approve] a savage, inhuman warfare, in which men are to be shot down like dogs, after throwing down their arms and holding up their hands supplicating [begging] for mercy."

But although some Confederate political and military leaders argued that the guerrillas were doing more harm than good, others defended their value. General Edmund Kirby Smith (1824–1893), for example, stated that Quantrill's raiders were "bold, fearless men . . . composed, I understand, in a measure of the very best class of Missourians. . . . [They] have waged a war of no quarter [mercy] whenever they have come in contact with the enemy."

In the months following the Lawrence massacre, however, support for the guerrillas faded as some of the bands became little more than murderous outlaw gangs. They terrorized civilian populations throughout Missouri in particular, even though Federal authorities repeatedly tried to stop them. By the spring of 1864, the entire state seemed to be filled with violent guerrilla groups. "The very air seems charged with blood and death," reported one newspaper. "East of us, west of us, north of us, south of us, comes the same harrowing [distressing] story. Pandemonium [wild uproar or chaos] itself seems to have broken loose, and robbery, murder and rapine [forcible seizure of another person's property], and death run riot over the country."

Quantrill, meanwhile, was unable to retain command of his band. During the last part of 1863 and the first months of 1864, some members of Quantrill's band quit in disgust over the massacre and other cold-blooded murders. These men had joined the company in order to fight the Union army, not to rob and murder defenseless civilians and terrorize families. As these men left, they were replaced by thieves and deserters who preferred the leadership of Quantrill's lieutenants. In the spring of 1864, Quantrill left the company after losing a power struggle with George Todd. He later formed another guerrilla group in Kentucky. Guerrilla groups in Missouri led by Todd and "Bloody Bill" Anderson, meanwhile, continued to use the war as an excuse to engage in widespread torture and murder.

Confederate guerrilla groups continued to operate through 1864 and the first half of 1865, but they became less effective during this time. As Northern victories piled up during this period, bands of rangers experienced the same drop in morale that affected regular Confederate soldiers. In addition, Union forces became more successful in tracking down many of the guerrilla leaders. Quantrill was among the bushwhackers who finally fell to Federal pursuers. Paralyzed by a Union bullet in May 1865, he died in prison a month later.

Famous American outlaw Jesse James once rode in William C. Quantrill's gang.

The Civil War finally ended in April 1865, after Confederate general Robert E. Lee (1807–1870) surrendered to Union forces led by General Ulysses S. Grant (1822–1885). Bands of guerrillas continued to roam through Missouri and other border states for the next several weeks, robbing stores and stagecoaches and killing pro-Union civilians. But several bushwhackers were killed in clashes with Federal soldiers and armed townspeople, and the groups began to realize that their days were numbered. Hundreds of guerrillas surrendered under a Union policy that guaranteed immunity (protection) from military charges but not from civil charges (charges brought by civilian legal authorities). Other guerrillas fled for Texas or Mexico, carrying faint hopes of establishing a new Confederacy. A few raiders turned to bank robbery and other criminal acts to support themselves. As the last of the bushwhackers faded away, the people of Kansas, Missouri, and other regions were finally able to begin the long process of rebuilding their lives.

Did you know . . .

- Many states sent men to fight on behalf of the Union, but Kansas contributed a greater percentage of its male population than any other state. This high level of volunteerism is usually attributed to the state's strong abolitionist beliefs.

- Quantrill's band of raiders included a number of men who later became famous outlaws in the American West. The Younger brothers—Cole (1844–1916), Bob (1853–1889), and Jim (1848–1902)—first became known around the country during their time as members of Quantrill's gang, and both Jesse James (1847–1882) and his brother Frank (1844–1915) rode with Quantrill at one time or another.

- Only one member of Quantrill's band of raiders was ever put on trial for the terrible massacre in Lawrence, Kansas. George M. Maddox was one of several guerrillas who had been identified by the town's survivors. In February 1866, he was captured and transported to the Lawrence jail to stand trial. Authorities agreed that Maddox would never be able to get a fair trial in Lawrence, so they moved the trial to Ottawa, Kansas. Despite eyewitness testimony about Maddox's involvement in the massacre, the jury deliberated for only ten minutes before announcing a verdict of not guilty. Most historians agree that the members of the jury were almost certainly bribed by friends of Maddox. In any case, dozens of Lawrence citizens sitting in the courtroom erupted in anger when they heard the verdict. Some of these citizens vowed to kill Maddox themselves. But Maddox slipped out of the courthouse's back door and galloped away with his wife before anyone could stop him.

- In the years following the Civil War, men who had been members of Quantrill's gang scattered all over the country. In September 1898, however, surviving members of Quantrill's raiders gathered in Blue Springs, Missouri, for a reunion. An estimated five hundred people attended the gathering, including thirty-five former guerrillas. Over the next several years, the reunion became an annual event that featured picnics, dancing, and sentimental speeches. These gatherings finally faded away as surviving members died of old age. Only five ex-guerrillas attended the last reunion, held in 1929. The last surviving member of Quantrill's raiders, Frank Smith, died on March 3, 1932.

For Further Reading

Brownlee, Richard S. *Gray Ghost of the Confederacy: Guerrilla Warfare in the West, 1861–1865*. Baton Rouge: Louisiana State University Press, 1958.

Goodrich, Thomas. *Bloody Dawn: The Story of the Lawrence Massacre*. Kent, OH: Kent State University Press, 1991.

Leslie, Edward E. *The Devil Knows How to Ride: The True Story of William Clarke Quantrill and His Confederate Raiders*. New York: Random House, 1996. Reprint, New York: Da Capo Press, 1998.

Schultz, Duane. *Quantrill's War: The Life and Times of William Clarke Quantrill*. New York: St. Martin's Press, 1996.

James Henry Gooding

A Black Soldier's Letter to President Abraham Lincoln
Written September 28, 1863

An appeal for equal pay for black soldiers

From the earliest days of the Civil War, free black men from the North tried to join the Union Army as soldiers. They cited two main reasons for wanting to fight. First, they wanted to help put an end to slavery. Second, they believed that proving their patriotism and courage on the field of battle would help improve their position in American society.

But Federal law prohibited black men from joining the Union Army, and many Northern whites wanted to keep it that way. Some whites claimed that the purpose of the Civil War was to restore the Union rather than to settle the issue of slavery. And since the war was not about slavery, they felt that there was no need to change the law so that black people could join the fight. Another reason that many Northern whites did not want black men to join the army was deep-seated racial prejudice. Some whites believed that they were superior to blacks and did not want to fight alongside them. Finally, some Northerners worried that allowing blacks to become soldiers would convince the border states—four states that allowed slavery but remained part of the Union anyway—to join the Confederacy.

> "We appeal to you, Sir, as the Executive of the Nation, to have us justly Dealt with. The Regt. do pray that they be assured their service will be fairly appreciated by paying them as American Soldiers, not as menial hirelings."

Black leaders in the North were outraged at the policies and prejudices that prevented them from fighting in the Civil War. Former slave and abolition leader Frederick Douglass (c.1818–1895) called it "a spectacle of blind, unreasoning prejudice" that government officials "steadily and persistently refuse to receive the very class of men who have a deeper interest in the defeat and humiliation of the rebels than all others. . . . This is no time to fight only with your white hand, and allow your black hand to remain tied." Many Northern blacks signed petitions asking the Federal government to change its rules, but the government refused. In the meantime, thousands of blacks provided unofficial help for the cause by serving as cooks, carpenters, laborers, nurses, scouts, and servants for the Union troops.

In 1862, the Union Army suffered a series of defeats at the hands of the Confederates. This led to low morale among the troops and difficulty attracting white volunteers. As a result, public opinion about allowing blacks to fight gradually began to change. On July 17, 1862, the U.S. Congress passed two new laws that officially allowed black men to serve as soldiers in the Union Army.

Black men finally got the opportunity to serve their country, but they still faced many forms of discrimination. For example, black soldiers were not allowed to be promoted to the rank of officer, meaning that they were stuck being followers rather than leaders. Black regiments (military units of organized troops) were always led by white officers. Black soldiers also performed more than their fair share of hard labor and fatigue duty, such as pitching tents, loading supplies, and digging wells and trenches.

In addition, black soldiers received lower pay than white soldiers of the same rank. Black soldiers with the rank of private were paid $10 per month, with $3 deducted for clothing. But white privates received $13 per month, plus an additional $3.50 for clothing. War Department officials claimed that black soldiers received lower pay because their regiments were used as laborers rather than as combat troops. In reality, however, thousands of black soldiers took part in battles and fought with great courage for the Union cause.

One of the most famous black regiments in the Civil War was the Fifty-Fourth Massachusetts. This regiment was or-

ganized by Massachusetts governor John Andrew (1818–1867) in January 1863. With the help of prominent black leaders and abolitionists, Andrew recruited free blacks from all over the North to represent his state. In July 1863, the Fifty-Fourth Massachusetts was chosen to lead an assault on Fort Wagner, a Confederate stronghold that guarded the entrance to Charleston Harbor in South Carolina. The troops charged forward through heavy enemy fire and reached the walls of the fort, but were forced to retreat when reinforcements failed to arrive. The commanding officer, Robert Gould Shaw (1837–1863), and nearly half of the six hundred members of the regiment were killed. But the regiment's bravery and determination in battle helped increase acceptance of blacks in the army and in society.

The Fifty-Fourth Massachusetts led a protest against the government policies that gave unequal pay to Union soldiers based upon their race. They refused to accept any pay

Black soldiers leave by train to serve in the Civil War.
(Courtesy of the National Archives and Records Administration.)

Massachusetts governor John Andrew organized the famous Fifty-Fourth Massachusetts regiment. *(Reproduced by permission of Archive Photos, Inc.)*

until they were treated equally with white soldiers. In response to protests from black soldiers and Northern abolitionists, members of the Republican Party in Congress sponsored a bill to equalize the pay of black and white soldiers. This bill proposed to make the equal wages retroactive (effective as of a date before the bill was actually passed), meaning that black soldiers would receive an extra $3 per month beginning from the time that they enlisted in the army. But members of the Democratic Party opposed equalizing the pay of black and white soldiers. Some Republicans questioned making the equal payments retroactive. Since the sides could not reach an agreement, the bill was not passed.

In some ways, being part of the Union Army was even more dangerous for black soldiers than it was for whites. Southerners were outraged when they learned that the North planned to allow black men to fight. They were especially angry that the Union Army would use former slaves—whom the Confederates considered to be stolen property—against them in battle. In May 1863, the Confederate government announced that it intended to ignore the usual rules covering the treatment of prisoners of war and deal with captured black soldiers in a harsh manner. The government issued a statement saying that captured black soldiers might be put to death or sold into slavery. Many people thought that the Confederacy was just trying to discourage blacks from joining the Union Army, but a few well-publicized incidents convinced other people that they were serious.

Confederate soldiers executed hundreds of captured black soldiers in the last years of the Civil War, as well as some white officers in charge of black regiments. One white Union soldier described what happened to black soldiers who were captured near Plymouth, North Carolina: "All the negroes found in blue uniform or with any outward marks of a

Union soldier upon him was killed—I saw some taken into the woods and hung—Others I saw stripped of all their clothing, and they stood upon the bank of the river with their faces riverwards and then they were shot—Still others were killed by having their brains beaten out by the butt end of the muskets in the hands of the Rebels."

Northerners grew angry and defiant upon hearing about such incidents. Union officials threatened to strike back using Confederate prisoners of war. "For every soldier of the United States killed in violation of the laws of war," President Abraham Lincoln (1809–1865) said in July 1863, "a rebel soldier shall be executed; and for every one enslaved by the enemy or sold into slavery, a rebel soldier shall be placed at hard labor on the public works." But Lincoln did not enforce this policy. One problem was that it would mean punishing innocent Confederate soldiers for the crimes of others. Another problem was that it would probably cause the Confederacy to retaliate in even more horrible ways. Instead, the Union Army stopped exchanging Confederate prisoners for Union soldiers who had been captured. These men remained in Union prisoner of war camps as a way of keeping the Confederacy from enforcing its policy of executing or enslaving captured black soldiers.

Under pressure from the U.S. government, the Confederates said that they would be willing to exchange captured black soldiers who had been legally free before the war began. But the head of prisoner exchanges for the Confederacy declared that the South would "die in the last ditch" before "giving up the right to send slaves back to slavery as property recaptured." Union officials would not accept this policy. The U.S. government refused to return Confederate prisoners until the Confederate government agreed to treat captured black Union soldiers—both freemen and former slaves—the same as captured white Union soldiers. In April 1864, Union general Ulysses S. Grant (1822–1885) declared that "no distinction whatever will be made in the exchange between white and colored prisoners."

In general, black troops were pleased and relieved that the Union supported them in the prisoner of war issue. But some questioned how the government could consider them equal to white soldiers if they were captured by the enemy, but still deny them equal pay. This is one of many questions raised in the following letter. James Henry Gooding, a black soldier from the Fifty-Fourth Massachusetts regiment, wrote the letter to President Abraham Lincoln on behalf of his fellow black soldiers in order to make an argument about why they deserved to be paid the same as white soldiers. He explains that the black soldiers are doing the same work as their white counterparts. He mentions specific battles in which black soldiers have fought with honor and courage for the Union cause. He also notes that black soldiers have willingly given their lives for their country.

Things to remember while reading James Henry Gooding's letter to President Abraham Lincoln:

- Toward the end of his letter to the president, Gooding mentions that he and the other members of his regiment are "freemen by birth" rather than former slaves. The Fifty-Fourth Massachusetts was unusual because its ranks were filled with free blacks from the North. Most other black regiments consisted almost entirely of former slaves. In fact, eight out of every ten black men who became Union soldiers during the Civil War were liberated or escaped slaves from the South.

- In some cases, slaves who became soldiers found it difficult to see any difference between their former masters and their white officers in the Union Army. The men placed in command of black regiments ranged from Northern abolitionists like Robert Gould Shaw (head of the Fifty-Fourth Massachusetts) to Kentucky slaveowners.

- Gooding talks about how black soldiers "have dyed the ground with blood, in defense of the Union, and Democracy." In fact, a black soldier was almost three times more likely to die than a white soldier during the Civil War. Black soldiers often experienced harsher working conditions than whites and did not receive equal access to medical care.

A Black Soldier's Letter to President Abraham Lincoln

Your Excellency, Abraham Lincoln:

*Your Excellency will pardon the **presumption** of an humble individual like myself, in addressing you, but the earnest **Solicitation** of my Comrades in Arms beside the genuine interest felt by myself in the matter is my excuse, for placing before the Executive head of the Nation our Common **Grievance.**On the 6th of the last Month, the Paymaster of the department informed us, that if we would decide to receive the sum of $10 (ten dollars) per month, he would come and pay us that sum, but that, on the sitting of Congress, the **Regt.** would, in his opinion, be allowed the other 3 (three). He did not give us any guarantee that this would be, as he hoped; certainly he had no authority for making any such guarantee, and we cannot suppose him acting in any way interested.*

*Now the main question is, Are we <u>Soldiers,</u> or are we <u>Labourers?</u> We are fully armed, and equipped, have done all the various Duties pertaining to a Soldier's life, have conducted ourselves to the complete satisfaction of General Officers, who were, if any[thing], prejudiced <u>against</u> us, but who now **accord** us all the encouragement and honour due us; have shared the perils and Labour of Reducing the first stronghold that flaunted a Traitor Flag; and more, Mr. President. Today the **Anglo-Saxon** Mother, Wife, or Sister are not alone in tears for departed Sons, Husbands and Brothers. The patient, trusting Descendants of **Afric's Clime** have dyed the ground with blood, in defense of the Union, and Democracy. Men, too, your Excellency, who know in a measure the cruelties of the **Iron heel of oppression,** which in years gone by, the very **Power** their blood is now being spilled to maintain, ever ground them to the dust.*

*But When the war trumpet sounded o'er the land, when men knew not the Friend from the Traitor, the Black man **laid his life at the Altar of the Nation,**—and he was refused. When the arms of the Union were beaten, in the first year of the War, and the Executive called **more food for its ravaging maw,** again the black man begged the privilege of aiding his Country in her need, to be again refused.*

Presumption: The act of going beyond what is right or proper, or overstepping boundaries.

Solicitation: An urgent request or plea.

Grievance: Reason for distress or complaint.

Regt.: Regiment; a military unit usually consisting of one thousand soldiers.

Accord: Grant or give something that is due or earned.

Anglo-Saxon: A white person of English descent.

Afric's Clime: Africa's climate.

Iron heel of oppression: Slavery; being held down by force.

Power: The United States government.

Laid his life at the Altar of the Nation: Offered to serve the country as a soldier.

More food for its ravaging maw: Additional soldiers to replace those who had been killed or wounded in battle.

Dusky forms: Dark-skinned bodies.

Mires: Mud.

James Island: An island near South Carolina where black soldiers fought and died.

Mould: Mold.

Fort Wagner: Confederate fort against which a black regiment led a Union attack.

Parapets: Walls.

Eloquent: Forceful, moving.

Paler hue: White skin.

Better acquaintance with the Alphabet: Refers to the fact that many blacks did not know how to read and write.

Rebel Chieftain: Confederate president Jefferson Davis.

Distinction: Difference.

Usages of War: Generally accepted practices of war.

Exacts: Demands.

Insurgents: Confederates.

Contraband Act: Allowed Union forces to seize property—including slaves— belonging to persons rebelling against the U.S., as "contraband of war"; such slaves were considered free and could join the Union Army.

Menial hirelings: People hired to perform lowly work.

Impetus: Incentive.

Flagged: Wavered.

Apathy: Lack of interest.

Spurned: Rejected.

*And now he is in the War, and how has he conducted himself? Let their **dusky forms** rise up, out [of] the **mires** of **James Island**, and give the answer. Let the rich **mould** around [Fort] **Wagner's parapets** be upturned, and there will be found an **Eloquent** answer. Obedient and patient and Solid as a wall are they. All we lack is a **paler hue** and a **better acquaintance with the Alphabet**. Now your Excellency, we have done a Soldier's Duty. Why Can't we have a Soldier's pay? You caution the **Rebel Chieftain**, that the United States knows no **distinction** in her Soldiers. She insists on having all her Soldiers of whatever creed or Color, to be treated according to the **usages of War**. Now if the United States **exacts** uniformity of treatment of her Soldiers from the **Insurgents**, would it not be well and consistent to set the example herself by paying all her Soldiers alike?*

*We of this Regt. were not enlisted under any "**contraband**" act. But we do not wish to be understood as rating our Service of more Value to the Government than the service of the ex-slave. Their Service is undoubtedly worth much to the Nation, but Congress made express provision touching their case, as slaves freed by military necessity, and assuming the Government to be their temporary Guardian. Not so with us. Freemen by birth and consequently having the advantage of thinking and acting for ourselves so far as the Laws would allow us, we do not consider ourselves fit subject for the Contraband act.*

*We appeal to you, Sir, as the Executive of the Nation, to have us justly Dealt with. The Regt. do pray that they be assured their service will be fairly appreciated by paying them as American Soldiers, not as **menial hirelings**.*

*Black men, you may well know, are poor; three dollars per month for a year will supply their needy Wives and little ones with fuel. If you, as Chief Magistrate of the Nation, will assure us of our whole pay, we are content. Our Patriotism, our enthusiasm will have a new **impetus**, to exert our energy more and more to aid our Country. Not that our hearts have ever **flagged** in Devotion, spite the evident **apathy** displayed in our behalf, but We feel as though our Country **spurned** us, now that we are sworn to serve her. Please give this a moment's attention.*

James Henry Gooding

What happened next . . .

The U.S. Congress finally reached a compromise in June 1864, nine months after Gooding made his appeal to President Lincoln. The War Department agreed to begin paying black soldiers the same wages as white soldiers at that time. Black soldiers who had been free before the start of the Civil War would receive an additional $3 per month retroactive to the time that they had enlisted in the army. The increase in pay for former slaves would be retroactive only to January 1, 1864.

Despite the discrimination in pay and promotion by the Union, and the threat of execution or abusive treatment if they were captured by the Confederates, more than two hundred thousand black men fought valiantly for the Union. By late 1864, black regiments made up about 10 percent of the entire Northern forces. Black men fought in almost every major battle during the final year of the Civil War. Approxi-

An 1862 law allowed blacks to join the Union Army. Here, the 107th U.S. Colored Infantry Guard stand near a shed in Washington, D.C. *(Courtesy of AP/Wide World Photos, Inc.)*

mately 37,300 black men died while serving their country, and 21 received the Congressional Medal of Honor for their bravery in battle. The courage and determination of black soldiers on the battlefield earned the respect of many white Americans and helped the North win the Civil War.

Did you know . . .

- Gooding is the only black member of the famous Fifty-Fourth Massachusetts regiment whose first-hand accounts of his days in combat have survived to this day.

- In addition to the Fifty-Fourth Massachusetts, several other black regiments found it necessary to protest against racist treatment within the Union Army. For example, in December 1863, a black regiment stationed at Fort Jackson in Louisiana revolted when they saw a black drummer boy whipped by a white officer. The officer was placed on trial before a military court, found guilty of "inflicting cruel and unusual punishment," and dismissed from the army.

- Although the U.S. government never officially retaliated against the Confederates' harsh treatment of black prisoners of war, Union field commanders did so unofficially on more than one occasion. During battles near Charleston, South Carolina, and Richmond, Virginia, Confederate troops forced captured black Union soldiers to build fortifications under enemy fire. This was a violation of the basic rules of war. Union leaders responded by putting an equal number of Confederate prisoners to work under similar conditions. In both cases, the Confederate officers gave in and allowed the black prisoners to return to safety.

For Further Reading

Cornish, Dudley Taylor. *The Sable Arm: Negro Troops in the Union Army, 1861–1865.* New York: Longmans, Green, 1956. Reprint, Lawrence: University of Kansas Press, 1987.

Higginson, Thomas Wentworth. *Army Life in a Black Regiment.* Boston: Fields, Osgood & Co., 1870. Reprint, New York: Penguin Books, 1997.

Litwack, Leon F. *Been in the Storm So Long: The Aftermath of Slavery.* New York: Knopf, 1979.

Williams, Walter L. "Again in Chains: Black Soldiers Suffering in Captivity." *Civil War Times Illustrated.* May 1981.

Abraham Lincoln

The Gettysburg Address
Delivered November 19, 1863, in Gettysburg, Pennsylvania

The president mourns fallen soldiers

The Battle of Gettysburg was a major turning point in the Civil War. It took place during the first few days of July 1863 on the outskirts of a small town in Pennsylvania. In the hills and fields surrounding Gettysburg, seventy-five thousand Confederate soldiers under General Robert E. Lee (1807–1870) faced off against ninety thousand Union troops under Major General George Meade (1815–1872). Both sides had a great deal at stake.

Lee had won a decisive battle at Chancellorsville, Virginia, in May, defeating a Union force twice the size of his own army. This victory increased the confidence of Lee and of the entire Confederacy. They believed that one more major win on the battlefield would turn Northerners against the war and force President Abraham Lincoln (1809–1865) to negotiate peace. Lee decided to invade the North in order to claim the victory he needed. He brought his Army of Northern Virginia into Pennsylvania in mid-June.

Meade knew that the legendary Confederate general was coming and moved his Army of the Potomac to meet Lee at Gettysburg. Meade's forces formed the last line of defense

"In a larger sense we cannot dedicate—we cannot consecrate—we cannot hallow—this ground. The brave men, living and dead, who struggled here, have consecrated it, far above our poor power to add or detract. The world will little note nor long remember what we say here, but it can never forget what they did here."

Lincoln Is Moved by His Visit to Gettysburg

The Battle of Gettysburg took place less than five months before Abraham Lincoln visited the town to dedicate a cemetery to the soldiers who had lost their lives there. As the president rode slowly through the town on horseback in a parade leading to the ceremony, he grew silent and seemed deep in thought. Along the parade route he saw bullet holes in buildings, the rotting corpses of thousands of horses killed in the battle, children selling shell fragments at roadside stands, and other reminders of the tragic events. "Throughout the fields of wheat and corn, across the orchards, over the hillsides, amid the trees—everywhere was the evidence of death: a shoe here, a belt buckle there, a dented canteen, a tattered vest, a torn picture of a child—scraps of men's lives scattered to the winds," Philip B. Kunhardt, Jr., wrote in *A New Birth of Freedom: Lincoln at Gettysburg.* "The men themselves were no more than mounds in the earth now, mounds with wooden markers and penciled epitaphs [words on a grave marker] upon them—inscriptions bleached by the sun, washed by the rain, hardly visible anymore: name, rank, unit."

After giving his speech, Lincoln spent some time with a local hero. Old John Burns, the town cobbler (shoemaker), had picked up the gun he used for hunting

The Pennsylvania State Monument in Gettysburg National Military Park. *(Courtesy of Kathleen Marcaccio.)*

squirrels and joined the Union troops in the heat of the battle. He used his skills as a hunter to take down many Confederate soldiers before he was wounded. As the Confederate forces advanced toward him, he threw aside his gun and pretended to be dead. He lay still on the ground overnight, then was rescued in the morning. Burns met the president wearing the same clothes he had fought in, complete with bullet holes, and the two men attended church services together.

between Lee and the Union capital in Washington, D.C. If the Union lost the battle, the Confederacy would gain access to Washington as well as other Northern cities like Philadelphia and Baltimore. It would likely mean the war would end in victory for the South.

Crowds gather in Gettysburg, Pennsylvania, in November 1863, for President Abraham Lincoln's cemetery dedication. *(Courtesy of the Library of Congress.)*

The two armies met on July 1. Although the Confederates made several attacks on the flanks (sides) of the Union line, the Union managed to hold its ground over the next two days. Finally, on July 3, Lee ordered a full frontal assault on the Union position. First he used heavy artillery fire in an attempt to destroy the Union defenses. Then he charged fifteen thousand men toward the middle of the Union line. But the Confederate troops had to cross a mile of open ground in order to reach the Union positions. The Union forces used cannons and gunfire to turn back the Confederate charge well before it reached them. Lee had made a terrible mistake that cost him the battle.

Union and Confederate soldiers lie dead on the battlefield at Gettysburg.
(Courtesy of the National Archives and Records Administration.)

The Union Army suffered twenty-three thousand casualties in the Battle of Gettysburg. The Confederates lost twenty-eight thousand men—about one-third of Lee's army. It was the bloodiest battle ever to take place in the United States. But it was also one of the most important. The Union forces pushed the Confederacy out of the North and proved that Lee could be defeated in battle. From this point on, Union soldiers fought with increased confidence and determination. When news of the victory spread, Northerners renewed their support for the war effort and for President Lincoln. Although the Civil War lasted for two more years, Gettysburg marked a significant turning point in the Union's favor.

Part of the battlefield at Gettysburg was turned into a permanent cemetery for soldiers who had died there. President Lincoln attended the dedication ceremony for the cemetery on November 19, 1863, and made a short speech. In what became known as the Gettysburg Address, Lincoln expressed his grief for the fallen soldiers, as well as his continued belief in the principles for which they had fought.

Abraham Lincoln's Gettysburg Address

Four score and seven years ago our *fathers* brought forth upon this continent a new nation, conceived in Liberty, and dedicated to the proposition that all men are created equal.

Now we are engaged in a great civil war, testing whether that nation or any nation so conceived and so dedicated can long endure. We are met on a great battlefield of that war. We have come to dedicate a portion of that field as a final resting place for those who here gave their lives that that nation might live. It is altogether fitting and proper that we should do this.

But in a larger sense we cannot dedicate—we cannot consecrate—we cannot hallow—this ground. The brave men, living and dead, who struggled here, have consecrated it, far above our poor power to add or detract. The world will little note nor long remember what we say here, but it can never forget what they did here. It is for us the living, rather, to be dedicated here to the unfinished work which they who fought here have thus far so nobly advanced. It is rather for us to be here dedicated to the great task remaining before us—that from these honored dead we take increased devotion to that cause for which they gave the last full measure of devotion—that we here highly resolve that these dead shall not have died in vain—that this nation, under God, shall have a new birth of freedom—and that government of the people, by the people, for the people, shall not perish from the earth.

What happened next . . .

The initial reaction to Lincoln's speech was mixed. Many of the fifteen thousand spectators who heard it that day were surprised that it was so short. Lincoln himself believed that it had been a failure. But once the Gettysburg Address had been reprinted in newspapers across the country and people

Four score and seven: Eighty-seven (four score equals 4 x 20).

Fathers: America's Founding Fathers, who led the country during the War of Independence in 1776 and created the U.S. Constitution.

Consecrate: Declare sacred.

Hallow: Make holy.

Detract: Take away.

Perish: Disappear or die.

had time to think about it, they began to express appreciation for his remarks. "Could the most elaborate and splendid oration be more beautiful, more touching, more inspiring, than those thrilling words of the president?" one newspaper asked.

Over the years, Lincoln's Gettysburg Address gradually became known as "one of the single greatest utterances [vocal expressions] in the English language," as Philip B. Kunhardt, Jr. noted in *A New Birth of Freedom: Lincoln at Gettysburg*. Many people only understood the true significance of the battle—and the ultimate meaning of the Civil War—after Lincoln explained these things in his Gettysburg Address. Lincoln's moving speech laid out the principles of democracy for which the North was willing to fight. "The war was not merely a test of the Union's cohesive strength, nor was it just a fight to end slavery and to extend the boundaries of human freedom. It was the final acid test of the idea of democracy itself," Bruce Catton wrote in *The Civil War*. "Gettysburg and the war itself would be forever memorable, not merely because so many men had died, but because their deaths finally did mean something that would be a light in the dark skies as long as America should exist."

Lincoln's address at Gettysburg introduced the idea of nationalism (a sense of loyalty and devotion to the country as a whole) into Northern debate about the Civil War. Instead of fighting to preserve the Union of fairly independent states with different interests and motivations, the North was fighting for the higher purpose of preserving the United States as a democratic nation. Lincoln believed deeply in democracy, which he described as "government of the people, by the people, for the people." He felt that if the South won the war and permanently separated from the United States, democracy would have failed. He encouraged people in the North to adopt this broader view of the meaning of the Civil War in the Gettysburg Address and later speeches.

Did you know . . .

- President Lincoln first heard about the Union Army's victory at Gettysburg on July 4, 1863—the eighty-seventh anniversary of the signing of the Declaration of Independence.

- President Lincoln almost did not attend the cemetery dedication in Gettysburg. His wife, Mary Todd Lincoln (1818–1882), begged him not to go because their youngest son, Thomas (Tad) Lincoln (1853–1871), was ill. But the president decided to make a quick trip from Washington by train and return the following day. His son was feeling much better by the time he got back.

- President Lincoln was not the featured speaker at the dedication of the cemetery in Gettysburg. Edward Everett (1794–1865), a well-known orator from Massachusetts, delivered the main address at the ceremony. He spoke for nearly two hours. The person in charge of the event, an energetic young lawyer named David Wills, merely asked the president to make "a few appropriate comments." Lincoln's response to this request ended up being one of the best-known addresses in American history. Afterward, Everett wrote the president a letter saying, "I should be glad if I could flatter myself that I came as near to the central idea of the occasion, in two hours, as you did in two minutes."

For Further Reading

Catton, Bruce. *Gettysburg: The Final Fury.* Garden City, NY: Doubleday, 1974.

Kennedy, Frances H. *The Civil War Battlefield Guide.* 2nd ed. Boston: Houghton Mifflin, 1998.

Kunhardt, Philip B., Jr. *A New Birth of Freedom: Lincoln at Gettysburg.* Boston: Little, Brown, 1983.

Montgomery, James Stuart. *The Shaping of a Battle: Gettysburg.* Philadelphia: Chilton, 1959.

Wills, Garry. *Lincoln at Gettysburg: The Words That Remade America.* New York: Simon and Schuster, 1992.

Edmund DeWitt Patterson

Excerpt from Journal of Edmund DeWitt Patterson
Written in 1863; first published in 1966 in *Yankee Rebel: The Civil War Journal of Edmund DeWitt Patterson*

A captured Confederate soldier records his thoughts

During the course of 1863, the fortunes of the two sides fighting in the American Civil War changed dramatically. As the year began, many Southerners expressed confidence that their struggle to gain independence from the United States would end in success. After all, the Confederate Army had won many of the major battles of the previous year, and Federal forces seemed unable to make any progress in their efforts to destroy the Confederacy and restore the Union.

In May 1863, the defiant South received another boost to its confidence when General Robert E. Lee (1807–1870) and his Army of Northern Virginia smashed a much larger Union Army led by General Joseph Hooker (1814–1879) at the Battle of Chancellorsville in Virginia. Lee's victory at Chancellorsville showed the Confederate general's continued mastery over Northern armies. But the triumph came at a heavy price for the South. Lee lost nearly thirteen thousand men in the battle. The best known of these soldiers was Confederate hero Thomas "Stonewall" Jackson (1824–1863), who was accidentally shot by his own men.

"Now, I am a prisoner of war on the little island of Lake Erie and with a prospect before me anything but cheering; entirely separated and cut off from the outside world, unable to take any active part in the struggle which is still going on between justice and injustice, right and wrong, freedom and oppression, unable to strike a blow in the glorious cause of Southern independence."

In the summer of 1863, Lee moved his army into the North. He hoped to seize needed supplies and scare the Union into negotiating a peace agreement that would grant the Confederacy the independence it wanted. But Lee's advance was stopped in the first days of July, when the Confederate Army suffered a crushing defeat at the Battle of Gettysburg in Pennsylvania. The South suffered another major defeat around the same time when Federal troops led by General Ulysses S. Grant (1822–1885) seized control of Vicksburg, a strategically important city located along the banks of the Mississippi River in Mississippi.

The nearly simultaneous Union victories at Gettysburg and Vicksburg changed how both sides viewed the war. The triumphs encouraged the North to believe that it might still win the war. At the same time, the outcomes at Gettysburg and Vicksburg triggered a wave of anxiety throughout the South. The weak Confederate economy became even further crippled by inflation (rapidly rising prices) and shortages of food and other supplies, and criticism of Confederate president Jefferson Davis (1808–1889) and his administration became extremely harsh in some parts of the South.

In the weeks following these two victories, the war continued to go in the North's favor. The Union armies pressed their advantages in size and firepower throughout the late summer and fall, attacking targets throughout the Confederacy. The rebel armies continued to fight very hard, and their victory at the Battle of Chickamauga in Georgia showed that they were still capable of defeating large Union forces. But by late 1863, the Union was putting constant pressure on the Confederate military, which experienced ever-growing problems finding soldiers and supplies for its armies. As Confederate losses mounted, Southern regrets about the war's horrible bloodshed and violence also increased.

During the last months of 1863, Union forces pushed through large sections of Confederate territory, seizing control of both small villages and big cities. This loss of territory worried and angered Southern soldiers and citizens alike. Each defeat seemed to increase the fury that Southerners felt about the "tyranny" (harsh or oppressive rule) of Abraham Lincoln (1809–1865) and the North. Many of them vowed that the Confederacy would never surrender to the North, no matter how bad the situation became.

But even though Southern defiance remained strong, growing numbers of people began to wonder if the Confederacy's only hope of victory lay in a change in Union leadership. They knew that Northern communities were sick of the war, too. They also knew that many Democrats in the U.S. Congress were calling for an end to the conflict, even if that meant granting the Confederacy its independence. As 1863 drew to a close, countless Southerners watched the political situation in the North with great interest. They thought that if the Democrats could gain enough power in the Federal government, they might grant the South its independence in exchange for an end to the war.

Many of the hopes and fears and regrets that Southerners felt in the final weeks of 1863 can be seen in the journal entries of a Confederate soldier named Edmund DeWitt Patterson. Patterson grew up in Ohio, but moved south in 1859 in an effort to carve out a living for himself. By the time the Civil War started in 1861, Patterson had come to view himself as a Southerner. Convinced that his adopted homeland was being mistreated by the North, he supported the push for secession from the United States. He fought under the Confederate flag until July 1863, when he was captured by Union troops at the Battle of Gettysburg. He spent the remainder of the war in prison, where he continued to keep a diary of his experiences and thoughts.

Things to remember while reading the excerpt from *Journal of Edmund DeWitt Patterson:*

- Patterson describes the war between the American North and South as a "struggle . . . between justice and injustice, right and wrong, freedom and oppression." These words reflected the widespread Confederate belief that the Civil War had erupted because of Northern arrogance and bullying toward the South.

- Patterson's journal entries reflect the Confederate view of the South as a region full of men and women of great courage and character. Many of its inhabitants also harbored a great love for Southern society and for the physical beauty of the land in which they lived. Their pride in their homeland became even stronger during the Civil War, when it was threatened by invading Yankee armies.

Edmund DeWitt Patterson

Edmund DeWitt Patterson was born in Lorain County, Ohio, on March 20, 1842. At the age of seventeen, he left school and traveled down into the American South, where he tried to make a living as a salesman. After a few months of selling books and magazines, he secured a job as a schoolteacher in Alabama.

Patterson enjoyed living in the South very much, and he became a strong believer in the region's right to secede from the Union if it wished. When the Civil War broke out in April 1861, he decided to enlist in the Confederate Army, even though his family back in Ohio strongly supported the Union. He became a part of the Ninth Alabama Regiment and spent the next two and a half years fighting for the South. Patterson participated in several major battles and campaigns during this period, including the Battle of Williamsburg (April-May 1862), the Seven Days' Battle (June 1862), and the Battle of Chancellorsville (May 1863). He also fought at Gettysburg (July 1863), but was captured during the battle's second day of fighting. His captors sent him to Johnson's Island, an island in Lake Erie located near Sandusky, Ohio, that housed many Confederate prisoners of war.

Members of Patterson's family lived only a few miles away from the prison, and they occasionally came to visit him. But Patterson did not always enjoy the visits. "[My father] urges me to give up the cause of the South which he pronounces a doomed one," Patterson wrote in his diary. "I can scarcely consider myself a member of the family—we have nothing in com-

- As the following excerpt shows, the Confederate Army was struggling with severe manpower shortages by the end of 1863. Historians estimate that the Northern states had more than twice as many men available for military service as the South. As the Civil War progressed, this advantage became a decisive factor. The Union Army suffered enormous losses during the war, but the size of the North's population made it possible for the military to resupply itself with thousands and thousands of new recruits. But the South had fewer men to begin with, and as the war dragged on, Confederate military leaders had great difficulty in finding new troops to replace soldiers who were killed, wounded, or captured.

mon." Patterson's differences with his family over the war caused a rift (break or division) that divided them for many years after the conflict ended.

Patterson spent nearly two years in prison before being released on March 14, 1865. He and three hundred other rebel soldiers were released in exchange for a large number of Union soldiers who had been captured by the South. Patterson prepared to rejoin his old army unit, but before he could do so, General Robert E. Lee and the rebel Army of Northern Virginia surrendered to General Ulysses S. Grant and his Union forces at Appomattox, Virginia. Lee's surrender ended the Civil War for all practical purposes.

In the years following the war, Patterson became a successful attorney and businessman in Tennessee. He also served as a state senator and a circuit court judge. In the early 1890s, he finally patched up his relationship with his family in Ohio. By that time, he had adopted a much different view of the Civil War than he had taken as a young man. "He considered [the war] a tragic mistake, and for the rest of his life did not care to discuss it or his experiences in it," stated his grandson, Edmund Brooks Patterson. "He would have no part in any effort to glorify or commemorate the 'lost cause' or in the reunions of old soldiers which were frequent and popular during his later years."

- Patterson expresses great sadness about the death of Stonewall Jackson, who died of injuries received at the Battle of Chancellorsville (May 1863). His statements reflect the depth of sorrow felt all across the Confederacy upon the famous military leader's death. Jackson's valiant (courageous) performances at some of the war's major battles (First Bull Run—July 1861; Antietam—September 1862) and his spectacular Shenandoah Valley campaign in 1862 had made him a beloved and respected figure throughout the South. In the days following his death, many Southern newspapers published long eulogies (speeches praising someone who has recently died) on Jackson in which they compared him to the greatest heroes and military leaders in all of history.

The death of General Stonewall Jackson was a tragic blow to the Confederate cause. *(Courtesy of the National Archives and Records Administration.)*

• When the Union Army seized important Confederate cities and regions in the second half of 1863, many war-weary Southerners began to feel that their independence depended on a Democratic victory in the upcoming 1864 presidential election in the North. They knew that President Abraham Lincoln, who was a Republican, was determined to continue the fight to the bitter end. But many Democrats had opposed going to war in the first place, and their party leaders had bitterly criticized Lincoln throughout the first few years of the conflict. By late 1863, Southerners like Patterson had embraced a desperate hope that Northern weariness with the war would enable the Democrats to defeat Lincoln in the upcoming election. "The enemy are exceedingly anxious to hold out until after the Presidential election," confirmed Ulysses S. Grant. "[Confederate] deserters come into our lines daily who tell us that the men are nearly universally tired of the war, and that desertions would be much more frequent, but they believe peace will be negotiated after the [1864] fall elections."

Excerpt from
Journal of Edmund DeWitt Patterson

December 31, 1863

. . . Now, I am a prisoner of war on the little island of Lake Erie [Johnson's Island, near Sandusky, Ohio], and with a prospect be-

fore me anything but cheering; entirely separated and cut off from the outside world, unable to take any active part in the struggle which is still going on between justice and injustice, right and wrong, freedom and **oppression,** unable to strike a blow in the glorious cause of Southern independence.

Now, the end of the war seems more distant than ever. Time only shows on the part of the **abolition government** a firmer determination than ever to **subjugate;** while on the other hand time only shows on the part of the South a stronger determination to fight to the bitter end, trusting alone to the god of battles for success at last. And we will succeed. Who will say that a country such as ours, rich in everything that makes a nation great and prosperous, a country with broad valleys unequalled in fertility by any others upon which the sun shines, a country abounding in natural fortresses and inhabited by eight millions of brave people determined to be free and willing to sacrifice everything even life itself upon the altar of their country, united as no people ever were before, I ask, who will say, in view of all this, that the South will not be free. I engaged in this war firmly believing that the South would be successful and now after nearly three years of war, I find that time has only served to strengthen that opinion. I believe that winter will pass and spring come again with its **verdure** and flowers—I believe it as I believe anything that I see around me,—the fair fields of the South may be transformed into deserts, and the places where now may be seen stately **edifices,** tokens of wealth and refinement, may be made as howling wildernesses, **Yankee hirelings** may occupy every state, every County in the South, they may occupy our state capitols and our seaport towns,—but our hill tops and **hollows,**—never. We will carry on the war even there.

During the year that is just closing, many battles have been fought and many, many thousands of the young men of the South have fallen. Their bones lie bleaching in the sun on the fields of Chancellorsville, Fredericksburg, Gettysburg, Vicksburg, Chickamauga, and in fact all over our land from the Potomac to the Rio Grande [rivers] may be seen the soldiers' graves. No sculptured slab of marble marks their last resting place, but they are not forgotten, and the memory of their deeds will ever be **cherished** by a grateful people, and the story of their deeds will be handed down from **sire** to son as long as noble deeds are admired and respected by mankind. When I think of the many thousands who have fallen in battle and the still

Oppression: Tyranny or abusive bullying.

Abolition government: The Union government led by Republican president Abraham Lincoln.

Subjugate: Conquer or enslave.

Verdure: Healthy green vegetation.

Edifices: Large or impressive buildings.

Yankee: Inhabitant of a Northern state or a Union soldier.

Hirelings: Persons willing to do unpleasant tasks in exchange for money.

Hollows: Small valleys.

Cherished: Felt or showed love for.

Sire: Father.

greater number who have sickened and died from disease during the year my heart is filled with love and gratitude to that God who has so mercifully spared my life until this time. . . .

*In a few short hours the year 1863 will be numbered with the years that are past. Its great events, its battles won and its battles lost, its fields of **carnage** and bloodshed, its mighty hopes and expectations, its fond anticipations, its sin and sorrow, its suffering and **toiling** are almost ended. They have passed before us, shifting scenes in the great drama of life, and as the year 1864 opens up before us, we will miss many actors who have figured **conspicuously** before the country, during the year. The one most missed will be Jackson. He is fallen. The places that once knew him will know him no more forever. Never has the army before or since been half so much affected as it was by his death. They could look defeat cheerfully in the face knowing that finally they would triumph, but when Stonewall Jackson died, a sad and solemn gloom seemed to hang over the entire army, and this feeling **pervaded** the hearts of all. We will always have to acknowledge the battle of Chancellorsville, though such a brilliant victory, dearly won by the death of this God-like man. Many have been swept from the stage of action and the cry goes up from many bleeding hearts, "Oh, Lord, how long?" Our brothers go halting by on crutches; our husbands, our fathers **languish** and die in the hundreds and thousands of hospitals scattered all over the South. And again the cry, "Oh, God, stay thy hand!" And still the war goes on.*

*We have met with many **reverses** during the year, but the spirit of our people remains unbroken, and always rises equal to the occasion. We are learning to bear misfortune, and we must expect to bear still more. I expect to see during the coming year a larger portion of our country subjected to Yankee rule than has been at any previous time. Our armies are growing smaller day by day, and we have not the men to supply the places of those who fall in battle. It seems to me that we should fight only when some decided and important result is to be obtained, and save men as much as possible. Meanwhile our people at home where the foe has possession should remain quiet, take no step toward forming a state government in accordance with Lincoln's directions* [in December 1863, Lincoln outlined steps that conquered Southern states could take to return to the Union], *treat all citizens of the U.S. as invaders and enemies, let them have nothing except what is taken by force, show no desire*

Carnage: Massive slaughter.

Toiling: Exhausting work.

Conspicuously: Prominently.

Pervaded: Filled.

Languish: Weaken or fade.

Reverses: Setbacks or changes in fortune.

*to have anything to do with the U.S. Government, and the Yankees will soon find that it will require a standing army in every Southern state to enforce their laws. A **great party** will be raised up in the North who will demand that the war shall cease, and it will cease. Such a party is growing now, and is becoming stronger every day. But enough, 'tis almost midnight and as soon as the New year comes, I must lay myself away on my **shelf.***

Union general William T. Sherman on horseback. *(Courtesy of the Library of Congress.)*

What happened next . . .

During much of 1864, it seemed that Patterson's wish to see Lincoln defeated in the 1864 elections might actually come true. Early in the year, strong Union armies under the command of Ulysses S. Grant and William T. Sherman (1820–1891) marched into Southern territory in order to destroy the major rebel armies still in existence. They pursued smaller Confederate armies under the command of Robert E. Lee and Joseph Johnston (1807–1891) all over the South, but they could never quite catch them.

Grant and Sherman became very frustrated, and they finally decided to turn their attention to capturing two important cities that were still in the hands of the Confederacy. They believed that the threat of losing the vital cities of Richmond, Virginia, and Atlanta, Georgia, to Federal troops would force the Confederate armies to meet them on the field of battle. As Grant's army marched on Richmond and Sherman's troops closed in on Atlanta, their strategy proved effective. Lee's Confederate Army was forced to set up defenses around Richmond and the neighboring city of Petersburg, while Johnston's troops rushed to protect Atlanta.

Great party: Great movement of peole.

Shelf: Bunk.

During the summer of 1864, the Union armies tried all sorts of different strategies to capture Richmond and Atlanta. But the Confederate forces turned back every attempt, sometimes inflicting heavy casualties on the Union armies in the process. By mid-summer, Northern communities expressed great impatience at the lack of progress and growing horror at the war's terribly high casualty figures. Lincoln's opponents in the Democratic Party took full advantage of the situation. Referring to Lincoln as "Abe the Widowmaker," they blamed him for the deaths of soldiers who had lost their lives in the war. They also claimed that Lincoln's continued efforts to restore the Union would extend the war for years to come.

As the 1864 presidential election drew near, most people believed that the Democrats' presidential nominee, General George B. McClellan (1826–1885), would defeat Lincoln. McClellan insisted that he would fight to preserve the Union, just as Lincoln was doing. But his fellow Democrats pledged that their first priority was to make peace. Most people across America viewed the upcoming election as one in which voters had two choices: vote for Lincoln and a continuation of the war to preserve the Union; or vote for McClellan and an end to the war, even if it meant losing the Confederate states forever.

Lincoln himself believed that he would lose the election, which was scheduled to be held in November. He told one army officer that "I am going to be beaten, and unless some great change takes place *badly* beaten." The president even sent a letter to leading officials in his administration telling them to prepare for defeat. Southern observers, meanwhile, expressed growing confidence that Northern voters would remove Lincoln from office. In early September, for example, the *Charleston Mercury* proclaimed that McClellan's election would "lead to our peace and our independence . . . [provided] that for the next two months we hold our own and prevent military success by our foes."

But in the final weeks before the November election, the Union Army racked up a number of important victories that dramatically increased support for Lincoln and his war policies. First, the Union Navy won a dramatic battle at Mobile Bay, Alabama. Then, the Confederate stronghold of Atlanta fell to Sherman's troops after a siege of several weeks. Finally, Union cavalry forces under the command of General

Philip Sheridan (1831–1888) won a number of important battles in the Shenandoah Valley. These victories convinced Northern voters that restoration of the Union was near. They responded by reelecting Lincoln to the White House by a comfortable margin.

Lincoln's victory was viewed by most Union soldiers as very good news. Despite the many hardships and violent battles that they had endured, most Union troops interpreted Sherman's capture of Atlanta and Sheridan's triumphs in the Shenandoah Valley as convincing evidence that they were on the verge of total victory. One New York infantry soldier spoke for many Federal troops when he called Lincoln's win "a grand moral victory gained over the combined forces of slavery, disunion, treason, [and] tyranny."

Down in the South, meanwhile, Lincoln's reelection sent a wave of gloom and despair over the entire region. To many Southerners, a McClellan victory had come to seem like

Confederate prisoners are guarded at a Union camp in the Shenandoah Valley.
(Courtesy of the National Archives and Records Administration.)

the Confederacy's last hope for independence. News of his defeat made war-weary civilians and battered soldiers even more depressed about their future.

Did you know . . .

- Both Union and Confederate soldiers often compared themselves to the patriots who fought for independence from England in the American Revolution in 1776. Northern and Southern schoolchildren alike were raised in households that honored America's "Founding Fathers" (the men who signed the Declaration of Independence and led the country during the Revolution) as men of high ideals and great bravery. When the war broke out, both sides insisted that they were fighting for the same causes as had those revolutionary leaders. Confederates claimed that they were fighting to achieve independence from a tyrannical government, just as America had done back in the Revolutionary War. Pro-Union people, however, claimed that they were honoring America's Founding Fathers because they were fighting to preserve the nation that had been established by them.

- Lincoln received 78 percent of the Union soldiers' vote in the 1864 election, even though McClellan remained very popular with Federal troops who had served under him earlier in the war. But many of these soldiers indicated that McClellan's connection with antiwar Democrats made it impossible for them to vote for him. In addition, the long Civil War struggle had created a strong bond between Lincoln and many of his soldiers, who were determined to keep fighting until the Union was restored. "I had rather stay out here a lifetime (much as I dislike it) than consent to a division of our country," wrote one Union soldier who voted for Lincoln. "We all want peace, but none *any* but an *honorable* one."

- Most Union soldiers were permitted to vote at the camp at which they were stationed rather than travel hundreds of miles back to their home states. Three states controlled by Democratic legislatures, however, refused to allow soldiers to vote with absentee ballots (ballots that are submitted by voters located far away from the place where they are registered). The lawmakers in these states—Indiana, Illinois, and New Jersey—feared that most soldiers would vote for Lincoln, so they wanted to make it very hard for them to vote. Some Union generals responded to this political maneuvering by arranging long furloughs (excused absences) from the army for their soldiers so they could go home and vote.

For Further Reading

Hattaway, Herman. *Shades of Blue and Gray: An Introductory Military History of the Civil War.* Columbia: University of Missouri Press, 1997.

Henderson, G. F. R. *Stonewall Jackson and the American Civil War.* London, New York: Longmans, Green and Co., 1898. Reprint, New York: Da Capo Press, 1988.

Hendrickson, Robert. *The Road to Appomattox.* New York: John Wiley & Sons, 1998.

McPherson, James M. *For Cause and Comrades: Why Men Fought in the Civil War.* New York: Oxford University Press, 1997.

Mitchell, Reid. *Civil War Soldiers: Their Expectations and Their Experiences.* New York: Viking, 1988.

Patterson, Edmund DeWitt. *Yankee Rebel: The Civil War Journal of Edmund DeWitt Patterson.* Chapel Hill: University of North Carolina Press, 1966.

Royster, Charles. *The Destructive War: William Tecumseh Sherman, Stonewall Jackson, and the Americans.* New York: Knopf, 1991.

Thomas, Emory M. *The Confederate Nation.* New York: Harper & Row, 1979.

William T. Sherman

Correspondence with the City Leaders of Atlanta, Georgia
September 11–12, 1864

A Union general responds to pleas to spare a city

11

L ate in the summer of 1864, the leaders of the Union Army made a change in their military plans. Before this time, they had concentrated on finding enemy troops and beating them on the field of battle. But they gradually concluded that this approach did not go far enough to bring a timely end to the war. Instead, they decided to adopt a strategy of "total war." This strategy involved confiscating (seizing) or destroying private property belonging to Southern civilians (people who are not part of the army, including women and children), in addition to targeting the Confederate Army and its military supplies. The Union leaders hoped that total warfare would break the spirit of the Southern people and make them lose their desire to continue the war.

Union general William Tecumseh Sherman (1820–1891) led an army of over one hundred thousand men in the western theater (the area west of the Appalachian Mountains) during this time. His troops spent much of the spring of 1864 chasing a considerably smaller Confederate force under General Joseph E. Johnston (1807–1891) through Tennessee and Georgia. Sherman wanted to claim a major victory in order to

"We must have peace, not only at Atlanta, but in all America. To secure this, we must stop the war that now desolates our once happy and favored country. To stop war, we must defeat the rebel armies which are arrayed against the laws and Constitution that all must respect and obey."

restore Northerners' fading faith in the war effort. But Johnston frustrated his rival by using a series of strategic retreats to avoid direct fighting with Sherman's larger army. This tactic enabled Johnston to keep his army together. By the time summer arrived, however, Sherman had pushed Johnston's forces to the outskirts of Atlanta, Georgia—one of the major industrial cities of the Confederacy.

Sherman was not the only person who had been frustrated by Johnston's evasive tactics. Confederate president Jefferson Davis (1808–1889) viewed his general's decision to retreat as an unwillingness to fight. Like Sherman, Davis felt that he needed a big victory on the battlefield in order to improve the morale of his people. So Davis replaced Johnston with Lieutenant General John B. Hood (1831–1879), a bold leader known for his aggressive style. Hood went on the offensive against Sherman's larger Union forces in mid-July. The Confederate Army suffered thousands of casualties (killed and wounded soldiers) in a series of battles around Atlanta. By August, Hood and his troops were trapped in the city.

Rather than attacking Atlanta directly, Sherman decided to lay siege to the city. He surrounded it with troops, cut off the Confederate supply lines, and began pounding the enemy forces with artillery fire. Finally, Hood was forced to evacuate his men from the city. The Union Army captured Atlanta on September 2, 1864, after four months of nearly constant fighting. President Abraham Lincoln (1809–1865) and others across the North were thrilled when they heard the news. Lincoln declared a national day of celebration and ordered 100-gun salutes in a dozen major Northern cities. The victory convinced many Northerners to renew their support for the war effort and for Lincoln.

When Sherman marched into Atlanta, he found that parts of the city were in ruins from weeks of Union bombing. In addition, Hood's retreating troops had blown up a supply train and taken all the valuables they could carry in order to prevent them from falling into Union hands. As a result, many of the civilians who remained in Atlanta had lost their homes and were having trouble feeding their families.

Sherman decided to stay in Atlanta for several weeks in order to rest and resupply his troops. But the general had seen what had happened when other Southern cities were

Confederate soldiers prepare to defend Atlanta against the Union. *(Courtesy of the National Archives and Records Administration.)*

captured and occupied by Union troops. In some cases, whole army divisions became bogged down in caring for civilian residents. Sherman knew that he could not feed the people of Atlanta in addition to his own army. He also knew that some Southern civilians accepted Union assistance and then turned around and acted as spies for the Confederacy. After considering these factors, Sherman decided to send a message to Confederate leaders and the people of the South. Under the Union's new strategy of total warfare, Sherman ordered all civilians to leave the city of Atlanta immediately.

Sherman's order was controversial, especially in the South. Southern newspapers called the Union general the "chief among savages" and the "foremost villain in the world" for what they considered his cruel and unfair treatment of civilians in Atlanta. Prominent officials from both the city and the Confederacy protested against the order. But Sherman believed that this measure was both necessary and right. "If the people raise a howl against my barbarity and cruelty, I will answer that war is war, and not popularity-seeking," he stated. "If they want peace, they and their relatives must stop the war."

The following letters highlight the debate that took place over Sherman's decision to evacuate the civilian population from Atlanta. The first one is a letter addressed to Sherman from Atlanta mayor James M. Calhoun (1811–1875) and two members of the city council, E. E. Rawsom (1818–1893) and S. C. Wells. These representatives of the local government describe some of the hardships the residents will suffer under Sherman's order and ask the general to reconsider. The second letter is Sherman's response to the people of Atlanta, through their elected representatives. The Union general explains the reasoning behind the strategy of total warfare. He recognizes that his order will cause some people to suffer, but he intends to enforce it anyway in hopes of bringing a quicker end to the war.

Things to remember while reading General Sherman's correspondence with the city leaders of Atlanta:

- In his letter, Sherman tries to tell the people of Atlanta why they must leave the city, but does so without revealing his military strategy. "I cannot impart to [tell] you what we propose to do," he writes, "but I assert that our military plans make it necessary for the inhabitants to go away." Two months later, Union troops set fire to the city in order to destroy everything that could possibly be used by the Confederates.

- Sherman knows that the Confederates are outraged by his treatment of Southern civilians. But he claims that the Confederates have been practicing total warfare for some time, with terrible consequences for Union supporters in the border states (states that allowed slavery but still remained loyal to the Union). "I myself have seen in Missouri, Kentucky, Tennessee, and Mississippi, hundreds and thousands of women and children fleeing from your armies and desperadoes [reckless and dangerous criminals], hungry and with bleeding feet," he writes.

Letter from the city leaders of Atlanta to General Sherman:

Atlanta, Georgia, September 11, 1864

Major-General W. T. Sherman.

*Sir: We the undersigned, Mayor and two of the Council for the city of Atlanta, for the time being the only legal **organ** of the people of the said city, to express their wants and wishes, ask leave most earnestly but respectfully to **petition** you to reconsider the order requiring them to leave Atlanta.*

*At first view, it struck us that the **measure** would involve extraordinary hardship and loss, but since we have seen the practical execution of it so far as it has progressed, and the individual condition of the people, and heard their statements as to the inconveniences, loss, and suffering attending it, we are satisfied that the amount of it will involve in the **aggregate** consequences appalling and heart-rending.*

*Many poor women are in advanced state of pregnancy, others now having young children, and whose husbands for the greater part are either in the army, prisoners, or dead. Some say: "I have such a one sick at my house; who will wait on them when I am gone?" Others say: "What are we to do? We have no house to go to, and no means to buy, build, or rent any; no parents, relatives, or friends, to go to." Another says: "I will try and take this or that article of property, but such and such things I must leave behind, though I need them much." We reply to them: "General Sherman will carry your property to **Rough and Ready**, and General Hood will take it thence on." And they will reply to that: "But I want to leave the railroad at such a place, and cannot get **conveyance** from there on."*

We only refer to a few facts, to try to illustrate in part how this measure will operate in practice. As you advanced, the people north of this fell back; and before your arrival here, a large portion of the

William T. Sherman.
(Photograph by Mathew Brady. Courtesy of the Library of Congress.)

Organ: A group with a specialized function.

Petition: Make a solemn request.

Measure: Order.

Aggregate: As a whole.

Rough and Ready: The next railroad station south of Atlanta, where a neutral camp was located.

Conveyance: A means of transportation.

people had retired south, so that the country south of this is already crowded, and without houses enough to **accommodate** the people, and we are informed that many are now staying in churches and other out-buildings.

This being so, how is it possible for the people still here (mostly women and children) to find any shelter? And how can they live through the winter in the woods—no shelter or **subsistence**, in the midst of strangers who know them not, and without the power to assist them much, if they were willing to do so?

This is but a **feeble** picture of the consequences of this measure. You know the **woe**, the horrors, and the suffering, cannot be described by words; imagination can only conceive of it, and we ask you to take these things into consideration.

We know your mind and time are constantly occupied with the duties of your command, which almost **deters** us from asking your attention to this matter, but thought it might be that you had not considered this subject in all its awful consequences, and that on more reflection you, we hope, would not make this people an **exception to all mankind**, for we know of no such instance ever having occurred—surely never in the United States—and what has this helpless people done, that they should be driven from their homes, to wander strangers and outcasts, and exiles, and to **subsist** on charity?

We do not know as yet the number of people still here; of those who are here, we are satisfied a respectable number, if allowed to remain at home, could subsist for several months without assistance, and a respectable number for a much longer time, and who might not need assistance at any time.

In conclusion, we most earnestly and solemnly petition you to reconsider this order, or modify it, and **suffer** this unfortunate people to remain at home, and enjoy what little means they have.

Respectfully submitted:

James M. Calhoun, Mayor.

E. E. Rawson, Councilman.

S. C. Wells, Councilman.

Accommodate: Provide space for.

Subsistence: Food and other minimum necessities of life.

Feeble: Inadequate or incomplete.

Woe: Deep suffering; terrible trouble.

Deters: Prevents or discourages.

Exception to all mankind: Different from all other people.

Subsist: Continue to exist or find the means of existing.

Suffer: Allow.

Reply from
General Sherman to the city leaders of Atlanta:

Headquarters Military Division of the Mississippi, in the Field

Atlanta, Georgia, September 12, 1864

James M. Calhoun, Mayor, E. E. Rawson and S. C. Wells, representing City Council of Atlanta.

*Gentlemen: I have your letter of the 11th, in the nature of a petition to **revoke** my orders removing all the inhabitants from Atlanta. I have read it carefully, and give full credit to your statements of the distress that will be **occasioned**, and yet shall not revoke my orders, because they were not designed to meet the **humanities** of the case, but to prepare for the future struggles in which millions of good people outside of Atlanta have a deep interest. We must have peace, not only at Atlanta, but in all America. To secure this, we must stop the war that now **desolates** our once happy and favored country. To stop war, we must defeat the rebel armies which are **arrayed** against the laws and Constitution that all must respect and obey. To defeat those armies, we must prepare the way to reach them in their **recesses**, provided with the arms and instruments which enable us to accomplish our purpose. Now, I know the **vindictive** nature of our enemy, that we may have many years of military operations from this quarter; and, therefore, deem it wise and **prudent** to prepare in time. The use of Atlanta for warlike purposes is inconsistent with its character as a home for families. There will be no manufactures, **commerce**, or agriculture here, for the maintenance of families, and sooner or later **want** will compel the inhabitants to go. Why not go now, when all the arrangements are completed for the transfer, instead of waiting till the **plunging** shot of contending armies will renew the scenes of the past month? Of course, I do not **apprehend** any such thing at this moment, but you do not suppose this army will be here until the war is over. I cannot discuss this subject with you fairly, because I cannot **impart** to you what we propose to do, but I assert that our military plans make it necessary for the inhabitants to go away, and I can only renew my offer of services to make their **exodus** in any direction as easy and comfortable as possible.*

*You cannot **qualify** war in harsher terms than I will. War is cruelty, and you cannot refine it; and those who brought war into our country deserve all the curses and **maledictions** a people can pour out. I know I had no hand in making this war, and I know I will make more sacrifices to-day than any of you to secure peace. But*

Revoke: Take back or cancel.

Occasioned: Caused or brought about.

Humanities: Human aspects.

Desolates: Destroys; makes lifeless.

Arrayed: Grouped or arranged in order.

Recesses: Secret hiding places.

Vindictive: Vengeful.

Prudent: Characterized by good judgement.

Commerce: Business transactions; the buying and selling of goods.

Want: Extreme poverty or need.

Plunging: Unexpected.

Apprehend: Anticipate or foresee.

Impart: Disclose or reveal.

Exodus: Mass departure.

Qualify: Describe or characterize.

Maledictions: Curses or harsh condemnations.

William T. Sherman

Reap: Obtain or gather.

Torrent: Violent outpouring.

Desolation: Ruin or devastation.

Inevitable: Unavoidable.

Perpetuated: Continued or made to last indefinitely.

Improvements: Roads, buildings, and other man-made additions that make land more valuable.

Heretofore: Up to this point.

Compact: Agreement between states or individuals.

Relinquished: Given up; let go.

Jot: Tiny bit.

Tittle: Very small part or amount.

Provocation: Something that arouses strong feelings or stimulates action.

Desperadoes: Confederate guerrilla fighters; bold and violent outlaws.

Deprecate: Express disapproval toward.

Moulded: Made.

you cannot have peace and a division of our country. If the United States submits to a division now, it will not stop, but will go on until we **reap** *the fate of Mexico, which is eternal war. The United States does and must assert its authority, wherever it once had power; for, if it relaxes one bit to pressure, it is gone, and I believe that such is the national feeling. This feeling assumes various shapes, but always comes back to that of Union. Once admit the Union, once more acknowledge the authority of the national Government, and, instead of devoting your houses and streets and roads to the dread uses of war, I and this army become at once your protectors and supporters, shielding you from danger, let it come from what quarter it may. I know that a few individuals cannot resist a* **torrent** *of error and passion, such as swept the South into rebellion, but you can point out, so that we may know those who desire a government, and those who insist on war and its* **desolation.** *You might as well appeal against the thunder-storm as against these terrible hardships of war. They are* **inevitable,** *and the only way the people of Atlanta can hope once more to live in peace and quiet at home, is to stop the war, which can only be done by admitting that it began in error and is* **perpetuated** *by pride.*

We don't want your negroes, or your horses, or your houses, or your lands, or any thing you have, but we do want and will have a just obedience to the laws of the United States. That we will have, and, if it involves the destruction of your **improvements,** *we cannot help it.*

You have **heretofore** *read public sentiment in your newspapers, that live by falsehood and excitement; and the quicker you seek for truth in other quarters, the better. I repeat then that, by the original* **compact** *of Government, the United States had certain rights in Georgia, which have never been* **relinquished** *and never will be; that the South began war by seizing forts, arsenals, mints, custom-houses, etc., etc., long before Mr. Lincoln was installed, and before the South had one* **jot** *or* **tittle** *of* **provocation.** *I myself have seen in Missouri, Kentucky, Tennessee, and Mississippi, hundreds and thousands of women and children fleeing from your armies and* **desperadoes,** *hungry and with bleeding feet. In Memphis, Vicksburg, and Mississippi, we fed thousands upon thousands of the families of rebel soldiers left on our hands, and whom we could not see starve. Now that war comes home to you, you feel very different. You* **deprecate** *its horrors, but did not feel them when you sent car-loads of soldiers and ammunition, and* **moulded** *shells and shot, to carry war into*

Kentucky and Tennessee, to desolate the homes of hundreds and thousands of good people who only asked to live in peace at their old homes, and under the Government of their inheritance. But these comparisons are **idle**. *I want peace, and believe it can only be reached through union and war, and I will ever conduct war with a view to perfect and early success.*

But, my dear sirs, when peace does come, you may call on me for any thing. Then will I share with you the last cracker, and watch with you to shield your homes and families against danger from every quarter.

Now you must go, and take with you the old and feeble, feed and nurse them, and build for them, in more quiet places, proper **habitations** *to shield them against the weather until the mad passions of men cool down, and allow the Union and peace once more to settle over your old homes at Atlanta. Yours in haste,*

W. T. Sherman, Major-General commanding.

What happened next . . .

In the weeks following Sherman's controversial order requiring all civilians to leave Atlanta, wagons loaded with people and their possessions streamed out of the city. Union troops helped Southerners take bundles of personal property south to the Confederate line of battle. By late September, 446 families had been evacuated from the city, including 705 adults, 867 children, and 79 servants. About fifty families were allowed to remain in Atlanta.

After resting his army for several more weeks, Sherman ordered his troops to destroy everything in the city that could be used for military purposes. On November 15, Union soldiers set fire to manufacturing plants, machine shops, railroad tracks, and train depots. But the fires soon spread out of control. Flames engulfed Atlanta's main business district and moved on to residential areas. Union major Henry Hitchcock (1829-1902) described the scene as Atlanta burned: "Immense and raging fires light up whole heavens. First, bursts of smoke, dense, black volumes, then tongues of flame, then

Idle: Worthless or useless.

Habitations: Dwellings or shelters.

The ruins of a train depot after Union general William Sherman left Atlanta. *(Courtesy of the Library of Congress.)*

huge waves of fire roll up into the sky. Presently, the skeletons of great warehouses stand out in relief against sheets of roaring, blazing, furious flames." One-third of the city was eventually destroyed, including between four thousand and five thousand homes.

People throughout the South were shocked and outraged when they heard that Sherman's army had burned Atlanta. But Sherman continued to defend his actions. He believed in the concept of total war—warfare involving not only the official participants (the armies), but also the civilian populations of the warring states. He felt that defeating the Confederate Army on the battlefield was not enough to ensure a lasting peace. He thought it was also necessary to break the spirit of the civilian population that supplied the army and supported the war effort. Sherman believed that by showing ordinary Southerners the destructive power of war, he could make them want to surrender. "Sherman expressed more bluntly than anyone else the meaning of total war," James M. McPherson wrote in *Ordeal by Fire: The Civil War and Reconstruction*. "He was ahead of his time in his understanding of psychological warfare, and he was in a position to practice it."

As it turned out, evacuating and burning Atlanta were only the first steps in Sherman's practice of total warfare. After capturing Atlanta, Sherman "began to realize that the whole nature of the war had changed, and that a radical reconsideration of possible objectives might be necessary. He was in the very heart of the South, and he had subject to his orders many more soldiers than his foe could bring against him," Bruce Catton wrote in *The Civil War*. "He had broken the shell of the Confederacy, and—as he was to remark—he was finding hollowness within. His problem was to find the best way to exploit [make use of] that hollowness."

Sherman adopted a bold new strategy. He decided to march sixty-two thousand members of his army eastward across Georgia to the city of Savannah on the Atlantic coast. He would basically ignore General Hood's Confederate forces, which had moved north toward the Tennessee border. Instead, he would concentrate on waging total war against the Southern people. "If the North can march an army right through the South, it is proof positive that the North can prevail [triumph]," he wrote to General Ulysses S. Grant (1822–1885), head of all the Union

Gone with the Wind

The capture and evacuation of Atlanta form some of the most dramatic scenes in one of the best-known movies about the Civil War, *Gone with the Wind*. Based upon a novel by Margaret Mitchell (1900–1949), who won the Pulitzer Prize for her work in 1936, this epic 1939 film shows the tragic effects the Civil War had on the South and its people. Two of the main characters are Scarlett O'Hara (played by Vivien Leigh [1913–1967])—the daughter of a wealthy Southern plantation owner—and Rhett Butler (played by Clark Gable [1901– 1960])—a captain in the Confederate Army. During the siege of Atlanta, wounded soldiers and refugees from surrounding areas come pouring into the city. Residents are in a state of panic as Union artillery shells pound Atlanta's streets and homes. "The skies rained Death," one of the movie's subtitles reads. "For thirty-five days a battered Atlanta hung grimly on, hoping for a miracle. . . . Then there fell a silence . . . more terrifying than the pounding of the cannon. . . ."

After Union troops cut the last remaining railroad line supplying Atlanta, the Confederate forces decide to evacuate the city. Before they leave, they set fire to ammunition stores so they will not fall into Union hands. Terrified and desperate, some of the poorer citizens begin looting shops and taking all the food and supplies they can carry. Rhett helps Scarlett to escape the city before the Union troops arrive. They drive a wagon through the mobs and flames toward Tara, Scarlett's beloved plantation. The movie's subtitles explain what happened next: "And

Clark Gable as Rhett Butler and Vivien Leigh as Scarlett O'Hara in *Gone with the Wind*.
(Reproduced by permission of the Kobal Collection.)

the Wind swept through Georgia. . . . SHERMAN! To split the Confederacy, to leave it crippled and forever humbled, the Great Invader marched . . . leaving behind him a path of destruction sixty miles wide, from Atlanta to the sea. . . ."

Gone with the Wind won seven Academy Awards in 1939, including best picture, best director (Victor Fleming), and best actress (Leigh). The tragic romance between Rhett and Scarlett has captivated viewers for generations, and it remains one of the most popular films of all time. Many of the movie's details are historically accurate, including the names of the businesses in downtown Atlanta. But some historians have criticized the film for making the pre-Civil War South seem more glamorous than it was.

forces. "I can make this march and make Georgia howl!"

During this famous "March to the Sea," Sherman's army lived off the land, with no outside supplies or communications. Sherman spread his forces into a line that stretched sixty miles wide, and authorized them to "forage [search for and raid] liberally" for food and supplies. They cut through the heart of the Confederacy, taking whatever they could use and destroying whatever was left that could be used by the Confederate Army. The official army foraging parties were joined by groups of people called "bummers." These lawless groups followed along with the Union troops, robbing Southerners and burning their property for the fun of it. Sherman did not take steps to stop the bummers because they were basically doing what he wanted—waging total war.

Sherman concluded his historic march by successfully capturing Savannah on December 24, 1864. He was considered a great hero by the North and a horrible villain by the South. The March to the Sea claimed a great deal of food and other supplies that would have gone to support the main Confederate Army led by General Robert E. Lee (1807–1870). As a result, Lee's army existed on minimal rations and grew weaker. But perhaps more importantly, Sherman's march changed public opinion in the South against the war. Many Southerners, particularly in Georgia, came to believe that continuing the fight was not worth the cost Sherman forced them to pay. The Civil War ended in a Union victory just a few months later.

World War II general George Patton greatly admired Civil War general William Sherman. *(Courtesy of the Library of Congress.)*

Did you know . . .

- Sherman came up with an innovative way of destroying railroad lines so that they could not be used by the Confederates. First, his Union troops lit wooden railroad ties to create huge bonfires. Next, they laid the metal rails across the flames. When the middle of a rail became red hot, the soldiers twisted it into a pretzel shape known as a "Sherman necktie." It was impossible to straighten the rail without using a heavy milling machine. Sometimes the Union troops bent the rails around trees. For many years after the Civil War ended, it was still possible to see trees wrapped with Sherman neckties in the Georgia countryside.

- In the years after the Civil War ended, Sherman became close friends with both of his major rivals from the Atlanta campaign—Johnston and Hood. Johnston even helped carry the casket at Sherman's funeral.

- General George S. Patton (1885–1945)—one of the most famous U.S. Army leaders during World War II (1939–45)—admired Sherman and studied his military strategies. Some historians claim that Patton used some of Sherman's tactics during the Allied invasion of France in 1944, in which American troops successfully freed the country from German control.

For Further Reading

Carter, Samuel. *The Siege of Atlanta, 1864.* New York: St. Martin's Press, 1973.

Castel, Albert. *Decision in the West: The Atlanta Campaign of 1864.* Lawrence: University Press of Kansas, 1992.

Fellman, Michael. *Citizen Sherman: A Life of William Tecumseh Sherman.* New York: Random House, 1995.

Hirshson, Stanley P. *The White Tecumseh: A Biography of William T. Sherman.* New York: John Wiley and Sons, 1997.

Lewis, Lloyd. *Sherman: Fighting Prophet.* New York: Harcourt, Brace, 1932. Reprint, Lincoln: University of Nebraska Press, 1993.

Sherman, William T. *Memoirs of General William T. Sherman.* New York: D. A. Appleton, 1886. Reprint, New York: Library of America, 1990.

Walters, John Bennett. *Merchant of Terror: General Sherman and Total War.* Indianapolis: Bobbs-Merrill, 1973.

General Horace Porter

"The Surrender at Appomattox Court House";
excerpt from **Battles and Leaders of the Civil War**
Covering events from April 1865; published in 1887

An eyewitness account of Lee's surrender to Grant

12

During the first weeks of 1865, it appeared that the long and bitter Civil War between the North and the South was finally drawing to a close. The Confederate armies had fought valiantly (bravely) during the previous four years, but even the most optimistic Southerner had to admit that the war had swung in favor of the Union armies. In late 1864, Northern military forces won crushing victories in Mobile Bay, Alabama; the Shenandoah Valley, Virginia; and Atlanta, Georgia. After capturing Atlanta, Union general William T. Sherman (1820–1891) launched his devastating "March to the Sea." During this march through the heart of the Confederacy, Sherman's army wrecked tens of thousands of Southern homes and farm fields, shattering the morale of the South's civilian population in the process. Finally, the reelection of Abraham Lincoln (1809–1865) in November 1864 showed Southerners that the North supported his plan to continue the war until the Confederacy was completely destroyed.

Despite these many blows to their cause, however, the battered Confederate military continued fighting. In the West, small Confederate armies tried in vain to slow the

> "The terms I propose are those stated substantially in my letter of yesterday—that is, the officers and men surrendered to be paroled and disqualified from taking up arms again until properly exchanged, and all arms, ammunition, and supplies to be delivered up as captured property."
>
> *General Ulysses S. Grant*

progress of invading Union forces. In the East, meanwhile, the South's primary army—the Army of Northern Virginia, led by General Robert E. Lee (1807–1870)—maintained its defense of Petersburg and the Confederate capital of Richmond. They faced the Union's Army of the Potomac, led by General Ulysses S. Grant (1822–1885).

The South desperately needed to keep these two cities in eastern Virginia out of Union hands. But by March 1865, Lee knew he would not be able to defend the cities much longer. After all, sickness, desertions (soldiers leaving the army illegally before their term of service ended), and bloody fighting had reduced his army to fewer than fifty thousand troops. Union forces in the area had more than twice as many soldiers, with thousands of additional reinforcements on the way.

In late March, Lee decided that his army's only chance of avoiding complete destruction at the hands of Grant's forces was to slip out of Virginia and join another small Confederate army in North Carolina. He knew that losing Petersburg and Richmond to the Union Army would be a severe blow to the Confederacy. But he hoped that an escape might enable his army to continue the fight for Confederate independence.

On March 25, Lee ordered a surprise attack at one point along the line of Union troops surrounding Petersburg. At first, the assault seemed to work. Rebel soldiers poured into the area and seized a significant stretch of Union trenches. But the Union launched a powerful counterattack with infantry and artillery. Forced to retreat, the Confederates lost nearly five thousand men in the battle.

After this clash, Grant decided to press his advantage. On April 1, his Army of the Potomac seized the last remaining railway line that had been providing supplies to Petersburg and Richmond. The loss of the railway meant that already severe shortages of food, ammunition, and other supplies in the two rebel cities would shortly become even worse. Grant then ordered a full assault on Confederate defensive positions around Petersburg. This April 2 attack battered Lee's Army of Northern Virginia and convinced Confederate president Jefferson Davis (1808–1889) and his advisors to leave the capital. But the Army of Northern Virginia successfully held off the offensive until nightfall, when Grant called off the assault.

Grant hoped to keep Lee's army trapped in Petersburg and Richmond and finish them off the next day. During the early morning hours of April 3, however, Lee managed to take his forces across the Appomattox River. Before leaving Richmond, though, he ordered his troops to destroy most factories and bridges so that they could not be used by the advancing Federal troops.

During the day of April 3, Union troops assumed control of both Petersburg and Richmond. First, they put out the fires that had been set by the departing rebel soldiers and angry mobs of citizens. The Union troops then took up positions all around the city. On April 4, U.S. president Abraham Lincoln visited the conquered Confederate capital, escorted by a troop of black Union cavalry soldiers.

The sight of Lincoln and the black soldiers prompted tremendous cheers from Richmond's black population, who filled the streets in joyous celebrations of freedom.

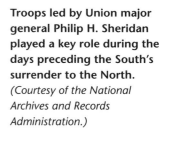

Troops led by Union major general Philip H. Sheridan played a key role during the days preceding the South's surrender to the North. *(Courtesy of the National Archives and Records Administration.)*

At the same time that Lincoln traveled through Richmond, Grant and his Army of the Potomac were engaged in a fierce pursuit of Lee's Army of Northern Virginia. Grant knew that if he could force Lee to surrender, the other Confederate forces scattered across the country would quickly follow his example. The exhausted rebel army did its best to avoid capture, but with each passing day Lee lost more men to capture, desertion, and Union sharpshooters. On April 7, Grant sent Lee a letter demanding that he surrender, but the Confederate general did not respond. A day later, Federal troops led by General Philip Sheridan (1831–1888) cut off Lee's escape route and captured two trainloads of food intended for the Confederates.

By April 9, Grant had completely surrounded the Army of Northern Virginia near a little Virginia town called

The McLean house in Appomattox County, Virginia, site of the meeting during which Confederate general Robert E. Lee surrendered to Union general Ulysses S. Grant. *(Photograph by Timothy H. O'Sullivan. Courtesy of the National Archives and Records Administration.)*

Appomattox. Trapped and exhausted, Lee realized that he had no choice but to surrender. One of his officers suggested that Lee might want to consider ordering his soldiers to scatter into the woods, where they could continue the fight as small guerrilla units. But Lee flatly rejected this idea. "[The guerrillas] would become mere bands of marauders [robbers], and the enemy's cavalry would pursue them and overrun many sections [of the South that] they may [otherwise] never have occasion to visit. We would bring on a state of affairs it would take the country years to recover from. . . . There is nothing left for me to do but to go and see General Grant, and I would rather die a thousand deaths."

On the morning of April 9, General Lee and General Grant met at a small farmhouse at Appomattox to discuss the terms under which the Army of Northern Virginia would surrender. Union General Horace Porter, who was a member of Grant's staff, offered the following remembrance of their historic meeting.

Things to remember while reading "The Surrender at Appomattox Court House":

- The Confederate Army of Northern Virginia and the Union's Army of the Potomac faced each other in many of the Civil War's most famous battles, including the First Battle of Bull Run (July 1861), Antietam (September 1862), Chancellorsville (May 1863), and Gettysburg (July 1863). In the first three and a half years of the war, the rebel Army of Northern Virginia won many of those battles. But improved military leadership and ever-growing advantages in manpower and supplies eventually turned the tide in favor of the Army of the Potomac.

- Many historians have said that the United States was fortunate that the Confederacy and the Union were represented by Lee and Grant at Appomattox. The two generals had fought desperately against one another for months. But when Lee surrendered, both men showed that they were eager to see an end to hostilities. Grant could have punished Lee's army for its participation in the rebellion against the Union. But instead, Grant drew up generous terms of surrender that eased the pain of the defeated rebels and made it possible for them to return home with some measure of pride and hope. Lee, meanwhile, resisted the temptation to order a campaign of guerrilla warfare that undoubtedly would have brought additional bloodshed and hatred to an already war-weary nation. As historian Bruce Catton commented in *The Civil War,* "In Grant, Lee met a man who was as anxious as himself to see this hardest of wars followed by a good peace. Grant believed that the whole point of the war had been the effort to prove that Northerners and Southerners were and always would be fellow citizens, and the moment the fighting stopped he believed that they ought to begin behaving that way."

- By the time that Lee and Grant met to discuss terms of surrender, Lee's Army of Northern Virginia was in very bad shape. His soldiers were exhausted and hungry, and they did not even have feed for their horses. As Porter recalls, Grant promptly made arrangements to deliver food to Lee's worn-out troops. Grant did this because he wanted to start healing the bad feelings between the two sides as soon as possible.

- One of the most important aspects of the surrender agreement was Grant's decision to allow Lee's rebel soldiers to keep their horses. Most of the long and brutal war had been fought in the American South, and many of its cities, towns, and farmlands had been destroyed. Lee knew that his soldiers' difficult task of returning to their families and rebuilding their lives would be much more difficult if their horses—used for both transportation and farmwork—were taken from them. As Porter explains, Grant quickly recognized how strongly Lee felt about this matter. The Union commander's quick decision to allow the rebels to keep their horses spared Lee the humiliation of having to beg for this favor.

- As Porter notes in his description of the surrender at Appomattox, General Lee was treated with great respect not only by General Grant, but also by other Union officers. They knew that Lee had been a brilliant commander for the South, and that he had fought for the Confederacy out of loyalty to his home state of Virginia. Even though they had spent the last few years fighting him, they viewed him as an honorable man who deserved courteous treatment.

Excerpt from
"The Surrender at Appomattox Court House"

General Grant mounted the steps and entered the house . . . while members of the staff . . . and some general officers who had gathered in the front yard, remained outside, feeling that he would probably want his first interview with General Lee to be, in a measure, private. In a few minutes Colonel Babcock came to the front door and, making a motion with his hat toward the sitting-room, said: "The general says, come in." It was then about half-past one of Sunday, the 9th of April. We entered, and found General Grant sitting at a marble-topped table in the center of the room, and Lee sitting beside a small oval table near the front window, in the corner opposite to the door by which we entered, and facing General Grant. Colonel Marshall, his military secretary, was standing at his left. We walked in softly and ranged ourselves quietly about the

In a measure: Somewhat.

Military secretary: Military assistant.

Ranged: Positioned.

sides of the room, very much as people enter a sick-chamber when they expect to find the patient dangerously ill. Some found seats on the sofa and the few chairs which **constituted** the furniture, but most of the party stood.

The **contrast** between the two commanders was striking, and could not fail to attract marked attention as they sat ten feet apart facing each other. General Grant, then nearly forty-three years of age, was five feet eight inches in height, with shoulders slightly stooped. His hair and full beard were a nut-brown, without a trace of gray in them. He had on a single-breasted **blouse**, made of dark-blue flannel, unbuttoned in front, and showing a waistcoat underneath. He wore an ordinary pair of **top-boots**, with his trousers inside, and was without spurs. The boots and portions of his clothes were spattered with mud. He had on a pair of thread gloves, of a dark-yellow color, which he had taken off on entering the room. His **felt** "**sugarloaf**" stiff-brimmed hat was thrown on the table beside him. He had no sword, and a pair of **shoulder-straps** was all there was about him to designate his rank. In fact, aside from these, his uniform was that of a private soldier.

Lee, on the other hand, was fully six feet in height, and quite erect for one of his age, for he was Grant's senior by sixteen years. His hair and full beard were a silver-gray, and quite thick, except that the hair had become a little thin in front. He wore a new uniform of Confederate gray, buttoned up to the throat, and at his side he carried a long sword of exceedingly fine workmanship. . . . We asked Colonel Marshall afterward how it was that both he and his chief wore such fine **toggery**, and looked so much as if they had turned out to go to church, while with us our outward **garb** scarcely rose to the dignity even of the "**shabby-genteel**." He **enlightened** us regarding the contrast, by explaining that when their headquarters wagons had been pressed so closely by our cavalry a few days before, and it was found they would have to destroy all their baggage, except the clothes they carried on their backs, each one, naturally, selected the newest suit he had, and sought to **propitiate** the god of destruction by a sacrifice of his second-best.

General Grant began the conversation by saying: "I met you once before, General Lee, while we were serving in Mexico, when you came over from General Scott's headquarters to visit Garland's brigade, to which I then belonged. I have always remembered your appearance, and I think I should have recognized you anywhere." "Yes," replied General Lee, "I know I met you on that occasion, and

Constituted: Composed or were the parts of.

Contrast: Difference.

Blouse: Shirt.

Top-boots: High boots.

Felt: A fabric made of animal fibers, like wool or fur.

"Sugarloaf": A reference to the shape of Grant's hat.

Shoulder-straps: Identification patch worn on the upper portion of the sleeve of a uniform.

Toggery: Clothing.

Garb: Clothing.

"Shabby-genteel": Worn clothing that used to be nice.

Enlightened: To inform or give information to.

Propitiate: To soothe or calm.

I have often thought of it and tried to recollect how you looked, but I have never been able to recall a single feature." After some further mention of Mexico, General Lee said: *"I suppose, General Grant, that the **object** of our present meeting is fully understood. I asked to see you to **ascertain** upon what terms you would receive the surrender of my army."* General Grant replied: *"The terms I propose are those stated substantially in my letter of yesterday—that is, the officers and men surrendered to be **paroled** and disqualified from taking up arms again until properly **exchanged**, and all arms, ammunition, and supplies to be delivered up as captured property."* Lee nodded an **assent**, and said: *"Those are about the conditions which I expected would be proposed."* General Grant then continued: *"Yes, I think our correspondence indicated pretty clearly the action that would be taken at our meeting; and I hope it may lead to a general **suspension** of hostilities and be the means of preventing any further loss of life."*

*Lee **inclined** his head as indicating his **accord** with this wish, and General Grant then went on to talk at some length in a very pleasant vein about the prospects of peace. . . .*

[General Grant then began writing the terms of surrender. He wrote very rapidly, but at one point, he paused and looked at General Lee.] *His eyes seemed to be resting on the handsome sword that hung at that officer's side. He said afterward that this set him to thinking that it would be an unnecessary humiliation to require the* [Confederate] *officers to surrender their swords, and a great hardship to deprive them of their personal baggage and horses.* [As a result, Grant wrote the surrender agreement so that Confederate officers would be able to keep their horses and personal possessions. After completing the terms of surrender, Grant handed them over to Lee for him to review.]

*Lee took it and laid it on the table beside him, while he drew from his pocket a pair of steel-rimmed spectacles and wiped the glasses carefully with his handkerchief. Then he crossed his legs, adjusted the spectacles very slowly and **deliberately**, took up the draft of the letter, and proceeded to read it **attentively**. It consisted of two pages. . . . When Lee came to the sentence about the officers' sidearms, private horses, and baggage, he showed for the first time during the reading of the letter a slight change of **countenance**, and was evidently **touched** by this act of generosity. It was doubtless the condition mentioned to which he particularly **alluded** when he looked toward General Grant as he finished reading and said with*

Object: Purpose.

Ascertain: Determine or find out.

Paroled: Released.

Exchanged: Handed over.

Assent: Agreement.

Suspension: End.

Inclined: Nodded.

Accord: Agreement.

Deliberately: Carefully.

Attentively: With interest.

Countenance: Appearance, especially facial expression.

Touched: Emotionally affected or moved.

Alluded: Referred to.

some degree of warmth in his manner: "This will have a very happy effect upon my army."

General Grant then said: "Unless you have some suggestions to make in regard to the form in which I have stated the terms, I will have a copy of the letter made in ink and sign it."

*"There is one thing I would like to mention," Lee replied after a short pause. "The cavalrymen and artillerists own their own horses in our army. Its organization in this respect differs from that of the United States." This expression attracted the notice of our officers present, as showing how firmly the conviction was **grounded** in his mind that we were two **distinct** countries. He continued: "I would like to understand whether these men will be permitted to **retain** their horses?"*

"You will find that the terms as written do not allow this," General Grant replied; "only the officers are permitted to take their private property."

A drawing by A. R. Waud shows Confederate general Robert E. Lee signing surrender documentation with Union general Ulysses S. Grant seated to Lee's left.

Grounded: Based or solidly placed.

Distinct: Separate.

Retain: Keep.

*Lee read over the second page of the letter again, and then said: "No, I see the terms do not allow it; that is clear." His face showed plainly that he was quite anxious to have this **concession** made, and Grant said very promptly and without giving Lee time to make a direct request:*

"Well, the subject is quite new to me. Of course I did not know that any private soldiers owned their animals, but I think this will be the last battle of the war—I sincerely hope so—and that the surrender of this army will be followed soon by that of all the others, and I take it that most of the men in the [Confederate] *ranks are small farmers, and as the country has been so raided by the two armies, it is doubtful whether they will be able to put in a crop to carry themselves and their families through the next winter without the aid of the horses they are now riding, and I will arrange* [the surrender agreement] *this way: I will not change the terms as now written, but I will instruct the officer I shall appoint to receive the **paroles** to let all the men who claim to own a horse or mule take the animals home with them to work their little farms."*

*Lee now looked greatly relieved, and though anything but a **demonstrative** man, he gave every evidence of his appreciation of this concession, and said, "This will have the best possible effect upon the men. It will be very **gratifying** and will do much toward **conciliating** our people."*

[Members of both generals' staffs began writing out the final versions of the surrender agreement. As they did this, General Lee brought up the subject of prisoners of war.] *"I have a thousand or more of your men as prisoners, General Grant, a number of them officers whom we have required to march along with us for several days. I shall be glad to send them into your lines as soon as it can be arranged, for I have no **provisions** for them. I have, indeed, nothing for my own men. They have been living for the last few days principally upon **parched** corn, and we are badly in need of both **rations** and **forage**. I telegraphed to Lynchburg, directing several train-loads of rations to be sent on by rail from there, and when they arrive I **should be glad** to have the **present wants** of my men supplied from them."*

At this remark all eyes turned toward [Union general Philip] *Sheridan, for he had captured these trains with his cavalry the night before, near Appomattox Station. General Grant replied: "I should like to have our men sent within our lines as soon as possible. I will take steps at once to have your army supplied with rations, but I am*

Concession: To yield or give in.

Paroles: Formal promises to honor certain conditions in exchange for release.

Demonstrative: Openly expressing emotions.

Gratifying: Satisfying; pleasing.

Conciliating: Reconciling or restoring good relations.

Provisions: Supplies such as food and clothing.

Parched: Dried or roasted.

Rations: Food.

Forage: Food for domestic animals.

Should be glad: Would appreciate.

Present wants: Current needs.

sorry we have no forage for the animals. We have had to depend upon the country for our supply of forage. Of about how many men does your present force consist?"

"Indeed, I am not able to say," Lee answered after a slight pause. "My losses in killed and wounded have been **exceedingly** heavy, and, besides, there have been many **stragglers** and some deserters. All my reports and public papers [and private letters] had to be destroyed on the march, to prevent them from falling into the hands of your people. Many companies are entirely without officers, and I have not seen any **returns** for several days; so that I have no means of ascertaining our present strength."

General Grant had taken great pains to have a daily estimate made of the enemy's forces from all the data that could be obtained, and, judging it to be about 25,000 at this time, he said: "Suppose I sent over 25,000 rations, do you think that will be a sufficient supply?" "I think it will be **ample**," remarked Lee, and added with considerable **earnestness** of manner, "and it will be a great relief, I assure you."

[After Grant and Lee signed the terms of surrender, they and their officers walked out to the porch.] Lee signaled to his **orderly** to bring up his horse, and while the animal was being bridled the general stood on the lowest step and gazed sadly in the direction of the valley beyond where his army lay—now an army of prisoners. He **smote** his hands together a number of times in an absent sort of a way; seemed not to see the group of Union officers in the yard who rose respectfully at his approach, and appeared **unconscious** of everything about him. All appreciated the sadness that overwhelmed him, and he had the personal sympathy of every one who **beheld** him at this supreme moment of **trial**. The approach of his horse seemed to recall him from his **reverie**, and he at once mounted. General Grant now stepped down from the porch, and, moving toward him, saluted him by raising his hat. He was followed in this act of courtesy by all our officers present; Lee raised his hat respectfully, and rode off to break the sad news to the brave fellows whom he had so long commanded.

General Grant and his staff then mounted and started for the headquarters camp, which, in the meantime, had been **pitched** near by. The news of the surrender had reached the Union lines, and the firing of salutes began at several points, but the general sent orders at once to have them stopped, and used these words in referring to the occurrence: "The war is over, the rebels are our countrymen

Exceedingly: Very.

Stragglers: Individuals who have strayed from or fallen behind a group.

Returns: Reports.

Ample: Plenty.

Earnestness: Honesty or sincerity.

Orderly: Assistant.

Smote: Clapped.

Unconscious: Unaware.

Beheld: Saw or witnessed.

Trial: A state of pain caused by a very difficult situation or condition.

Reverie: Daydream.

Pitched: Established or set up.

Abstain: Not do something.

Charges: Ammunition.

Furled: Rolled up and put away.

*again, and the best sign of rejoicing after the victory will be to **abstain** from all demonstrations in the field."*

[The following day, Lee and Grant met again to discuss minor details of the surrender. The two generals then returned to their respective armies to make sure that the surrender proceeded as planned. Grant and Lee then prepared to travel to Washington and Richmond to tell political leaders on both sides about the surrender.] *The hour of noon . . . arrived, and General Grant . . . mounted his horse, and started with his staff for Washington. . . . Lee set out for Richmond, and it was felt by all that peace had at last dawned upon the land. The **charges** were now withdrawn from the guns, the camp-fires were left to smolder in their ashes, the flags were tenderly **furled**—those historic banners, battle-stained, bullet-riddled, many of them but remnants of their former selves, with scarcely enough left of them on which to imprint the names of the battles they had seen—and the Army of the Union and the Army of Northern Virginia turned their backs upon each other for the first time in four long, bloody years.*

What happened next . . .

When other Confederate armies learned that Lee had surrendered, they laid their weapons down, too. All across the South, the tattered (torn and ragged) remains of various rebel military forces surrendered and returned to their homes to try and rebuild their lives. On April 18, Confederate general Joseph Johnston surrendered his Army of Tennessee to Union general William T. Sherman in Raleigh, North Carolina. Johnston's army was the last rebel force of any significant size left in the South, and his surrender made it clear that the Confederate nation no longer really existed. By May 26, all Confederate armies in the South had surrendered. Its soldiers scattered, returning to long-suffering friends and families. Upon returning home, they began the difficult process of rebuilding their lives out of the smoking ruins of the Confederacy.

Northern communities, meanwhile, recognized that Lee's surrender meant that the war was over for all practical purposes. Joyful celebrations erupted all across the North, as news of Grant's victory spread from big cities to the most remote homestead. Abolitionists expressed delight that slavery would finally be abolished from America, while Unionists sang and danced to celebrate the restoration of the United States. But most of all, people celebrated because Lee's surrender meant that the long years of violence and bloodshed were finally coming to an end.

A few days after Lee's surrender, however, Northern celebrations came to an abrupt end as one final act of violence shook the entire nation. On April 14, 1865, John Wilkes Booth (1838–1865) shot President Abraham Lincoln at a Washington theater, then escaped into the night. Lincoln died the next day. The assassination shocked the country and triggered an outpouring of grief and rage across the North.

Did you know . . .

- The meeting between Lee and Grant at Appomattox was delayed when they discovered that there was not any ink in the farmhouse in which they were meeting. Since the representatives of the two armies could not draw up any official terms of surrender without ink, officers on the staffs of both Lee and Grant looked through the building's cupboards and desks in hopes of finding some. After several minutes of unsuccessful searching, one of General Lee's officers finally stepped forward with a small supply of ink so that the terms could be drawn up.

- Of the fourteen bloodiest battles that took place in the American Civil War, ten of them were fought between the Confederate Army of Northern Virginia and the Union Army of the Potomac. In each of these ten battles, at least seventeen thousand soldiers were killed or wounded.

- After the Civil War ended, Robert E. Lee became president of Washington College in Lexington, Virginia. He served the college in that position until his death in 1870. After he died, the school administration formally changed the name of the school to Washington and Lee University in honor of the general.

For Further Reading

Catton, Bruce. *Grant Takes Command.* Boston: Little, Brown, 1969.

Dowdey, Clifford. *Lee's Last Campaign: The Story of Lee and His Men against Grant.* Boston: Little Brown, 1960. Reprint, Lincoln: University of Nebraska Press, 1993.

Horn, John. *The Petersburg Campaign: June 1864–April 1865.* Conshohocken, PA: Combined Books, 1993.

Gideon Welles

13

Excerpt from **Diary of Gideon Welles**
Covering events from April 1865; first published in 1911

A Cabinet member recalls the day President Lincoln died

In April 1865, it became clear to most Americans that the Confederacy was on the verge (edge) of total collapse. The Union's successful capture of the Confederate capital of Richmond, Virginia, in early April showed that no Southern city was safe from Yankee troops. Then, a few days later, on April 9, 1865, the South lost its largest and best army when Confederate general Robert E. Lee (1807–1870) and his Army of Northern Virginia surrendered to Union general Ulysses S. Grant (1822–1885) and the Army of the Potomac at Appomattox, Virginia.

News of these military victories raced through Northern communities. People across the North knew that such triumphs meant that the war was drawing to a close, and that the Union would be preserved. All across the Northern states, people poured out into the streets to celebrate. Laughing and crying in happiness, these crowds spent hours congratulating each other on the good news. Thousands of townspeople and villagers celebrated by firing rifles and fireworks into the air and ringing church bells, while countless others galloped or ran or paraded through the streets waving flags and singing

"The giant [Lincoln] sufferer lay extended diagonally across the bed, which was not long enough for him. He had been stripped of his clothes. His large arms, which were occasionally exposed, were of a size which one would scarce have expected from his spare appearance. His slow, full respiration lifted the clothes with each breath that he took. His features were calm and striking."

patriotic songs. "Never did so many flags wave in the nation's history, even though half the country wasn't waving any," wrote Robert Hendrickson in *The Road to Appomattox*. "Enemies shook hands and strangers hugged each other. Those against the war and those for the war all joined in rejoicing that the war was over, and all cried that Monday as they celebrated. People from every walk of life—from doctors and lawyers to foundry workers and porters—shouted: 'The war is over! Hurrah for Grant! Hurrah for Lincoln! The boys are coming home!'"

News of Lee's surrender gladdened the heart of President Abraham Lincoln (1809–1865), too. At times it had seemed to him that the war might never end, or that it would end in failure for the Union after years of heartache and pain. But Lee's surrender was a sure sign that Lincoln's heroic efforts to restore the Union had succeeded. When thousands of people gathered outside the White House to sing "The Star-Spangled Banner" and other patriotic songs, the president led them in raucous cheers for General Grant and his soldiers.

In the days immediately after the Confederate surrender at Appomattox, Lincoln spent a good deal of time thinking about how to bring the Southern states back into the Union. He knew that reestablishing a sense of unity and brotherhood between the two regions was going to be a big challenge. Lincoln realized that many people in the North wanted to punish the South for its actions. The president also knew that many Northerners did not want to readmit Southern states into the Union until they showed their loyalty to the United States and their willingness to honor laws that granted important new freedoms to blacks. But Lincoln believed that reunification would never work if the Southern states were not welcomed back with open arms. He wanted to give the Southern states significant control over their own affairs and help them rebuild their ruined cities and farmlands.

But Lincoln never got a chance to produce a comprehensive policy for reconstructing the rebel states and restoring them to the Union. On April 14, 1865, he and his wife, Mary Todd Lincoln (1818–1882), attended a play at Ford's Theatre in Washington called *Our American Cousin*. The Lincolns were joined by Major Henry R. Rathbone (1837-1911) and his fiancée, Clara Harris. Earlier in the day, President Lincoln had expressed little interest in attending the show. He even admitted to an aide that the only reason he agreed to go was because "it has been advertised that we will be there, and I cannot disappoint the people."

Upon arriving at the theatre, Lincoln and his party were seated in a fine balcony overlooking the stage so that they would have a good view of the play. Midway through the performance, however, a young actor from Maryland named John Wilkes Booth (1838–1865) slipped into the rear of the balcony, also known as the presidential box.

John Wilkes Booth was a fanatical supporter of the Confederacy, even though he never offered his services to its military. During the last few months of the war, Booth joined a small band of other anti-Union conspirators who devised several different plots to kidnap Lincoln. All of these plans fell apart for one reason or another, but Booth continued to plot against the president.

When Richmond fell, and Lee surrendered, Booth knew that the Confederate collapse was nearly complete. But he decided that if he killed Lincoln and other leading Union officials, the Confederacy might yet survive to fight. He also thought that if he carried out a successful assassination, he would be a famous hero throughout the South. This murderous reasoning led Booth to cast aside his kidnapping plans and concoct (invent) a new plot to assassinate Lincoln, General Grant, Vice President Andrew Johnson (1808–1875), and Secretary of State William Seward (1801–1872).

In order to carry out his scheme, Booth recruited a number of drifters, rebel spies, and deserters from the Confederate Army to his cause. Some of Booth's plan collapsed almost immediately, and the attempts on the lives of Grant and Johnson never even took place. But on the evening of April 14, one of Booth's accomplices (partners in crime), Lewis Payne, attacked Secretary Seward in his bedroom, where he was recovering from a carriage accident. Seward's son Frederick rushed to defend his father, but the secretary's son was seriously injured by the invader. Secretary Seward suffered numerous knife wounds, too, but he warded off his attacker until the man fled into the night. A few blocks away, meanwhile, Booth awaited the arrival of President Lincoln at Ford's Theatre.

John Wilkes Booth aims his gun at Abraham Lincoln at Ford's Theatre. *(Courtesy of the Library of Congress.)*

After entering the rear of the president's box at Ford's Theatre, Booth withdrew a one-shot pistol called a derringer from his jacket and shot Lincoln in the back of the head. Major Rathbone leaped to his feet to stop the assassin, but Booth slashed the officer with a knife and leaped out of the balcony, landing on the stage below. He broke his leg in the fall, but still managed to hobble to his feet. He yelled the state motto of Virginia, "Sic semper tyrannis" ("Thus always to tyrants"), at the stunned audience, then hurriedly limped off the stage to the rear of the theater. Rathbone called down to the audience and stage crew to stop Booth, but the assassin escaped on horseback before anyone could grab him.

Booth left behind him a scene of confusion and sorrow. Physicians in the audience rushed to Lincoln's side, but they could do nothing for him. Concerned that the president would not survive any attempt to carry him to the White House, which was more than six blocks away, the doctors de-

Gideon Welles (1802–1878)

Gideon Welles was a native of Connecticut who worked as a legislator and a newspaper editor for many years. A longtime opponent of the expansion of slavery into new American territories, Welles came to view the Southern states as excessively demanding and quarrelsome during the 1840s. In the 1850s, his anger about Democratic support for the slave states led him to switch his loyalty from that political party to the newly created Republican Party, which wanted to abolish slavery.

In March 1861, Welles joined President Abraham Lincoln's cabinet as the secretary of the navy. During the course of the Civil War, Welles proved to be an able administrator of the Union's naval forces. Aided by Gustavus Fox (1821–1883), the Union's energetic assistant secretary to the navy, Welles oversaw a dramatic increase in shipbuilding in the North. He helped the Union develop many innovations in naval warfare, and formed special committees to review strategic issues on the high seas. Finally, Welles presided (exercised control) over the creation of the Union naval blockade that strangled the Southern economy during the war.

Navy secretary Welles also emerged as one of Lincoln's more even-tempered cabinet members during the war. Welles adopted a more calm and cau-

Gideon Welles, President Lincoln's secretary of the navy. *(Courtesy of the Library of Congress.)*

tious attitude than many other officials in the Lincoln administration, and he was viewed as a moderating (not extreme or radical) presence in discussions of national affairs.

Following Lincoln's assassination in 1865, Welles continued to serve his country as navy secretary under President Andrew Johnson. He left office in 1869, after Ulysses S. Grant assumed the presidency. During his retirement, he wrote a number of books, including his diary and a book about Lincoln's relationship with Secretary of State William Seward.

cided to take him to a boarding house across the street from the theater.

As the evening wore on, many leading officials and lawmakers in Washington heard of the attacks on Lincoln and Seward. Senators and members of Lincoln's cabinet (a group of official advisors), including Secretary of the Navy Gideon Welles (1802–1878), rushed out into the night to check on the health of both men. Doctors attending to Seward assured visitors that the secretary of state would recover from his wounds. But physicians at Lincoln's bedside warned Welles and other officials that the assassin's attack had mortally wounded the president. Welles captured his thoughts and observations of the tragic historic event in his diary.

Things to remember while reading the excerpt from *Diary of Gideon Welles:*

- President Lincoln knew that the post-Civil War period in America would be full of challenges, as the North and the South tried to learn to live together again. Historians have offered a variety of opinions about the Reconstruction policies that he would have instituted had he lived. But most people agree that he would have favored moderate positions designed to: 1) address Northern concerns about black rights and Southern loyalty to the Union, and 2) make the South feel like a part of the United States once again.

- President Lincoln initiated many changes in American law and society that made life much better for black people. As a result, news of his death profoundly saddened black Americans across the country. They mourned his death not only because of his past leadership in abolishing slavery across the nation, but also because they felt that it made their future much more uncertain.

Excerpt from Diary of Gideon Welles

I had retired to bed about half past-ten on the evening of the 14th of April, and was just getting asleep when Mrs. Welles, my wife, said some one was at our door. Sitting up in bed, I heard a voice twice call to John, my son, whose sleeping-room was on the second floor directly over the front entrance. I arose at once and raised a window, when my messenger, James Smith, called to me that Mr. Lincoln, the President, had been shot, and said Secretary Seward and his son, Assistant Secretary Frederick Seward, were assassinated. James was much alarmed and excited. I told him his story was very **incoherent** and **improbable**, that he was associating men who were not together and liable to attack at the same time. "Where," I inquired, "was the President when shot?" James said he was at Ford's Theatre on 10th Street. "Well," said I, "Secretary Seward is an invalid in bed in his house yonder on 15th Street." James said he had been there, stopped in at the house to make inquiry before alarming me.

I immediately dressed myself, and, against the earnest **remonstrance** and appeals of my wife, went directly to Mr. Seward's, whose residence was on the east side of the square. . . . James accompanied me. As we were crossing 15th Street, I saw four or five men in earnest **consultation,** standing under the lamp on the corner by St. John's Church. Before I had got half across the street, the lamp was suddenly extinguished and the **knot** of persons rapidly **dispersed.** For a moment, and but a moment I was **disconcerted** to find myself in darkness, but recollecting that it was late and about time for the moon to rise, I proceeded on, not having lost five steps, merely making a pause without stopping. Hurrying forward into 15th Street, I found it pretty full of people, especially so near the residence of Secretary Seward, where there were many soldiers as well as citizens already gathered.

Entering the house, I found the lower hall and office full of persons, and among them most of the foreign **legations,** all anxiously inquiring what truth there was in the horrible rumors afloat. I replied that my object was to **ascertain** the facts. Proceeding through the hall to the stairs, I found one, and I think two, of the servants there holding the crowd in check. The servants were frightened and appeared relieved to see me. I hastily asked what truth there was in the story that an assassin or assassins had entered the house and assaulted the Secretary. They said it was true, and that Mr. Frederick was also badly injured. They wished me to go up, but no others. . . . As I entered, I met Miss Fanny Seward [Seward's wife], with whom I exchanged a single word, and proceeded to the foot of the bed. Dr. Verdi and, I think, two others were there. The bed was saturated

Incoherent: Confused or disordered.

Improbable: Unlikely.

Remonstrance: Protest or complaint.

Consultation: Conversation.

Knot: Crowd.

Dispersed: Scattered in all directions.

Disconcerted: Upset or confused.

Legations: Diplomats or representatives.

Ascertain: Find out or discover.

*with blood. The Secretary was lying on his back, the upper part of his head covered by a cloth, which extended down over his eyes. His mouth was open, the lower jaw dropping down. I exchanged a few whispered words with Dr. V. Secretary [of War Edwin] Stanton, who came after but almost simultaneously with me, made inquiries in a louder tone till **admonished** by a word from one of the physicians. We almost immediately withdrew and went into the adjoining front room, where lay Frederick Seward. His eyes were open but he did not move them, nor a limb, nor did he speak. Doctor White, who was in attendance, told me he was unconscious and more dangerously injured than his father.*

As we descended the stairs, I asked Stanton what he had heard in regard to the President that was reliable. He said the President was shot at Ford's Theatre, that he had seen a man who was present and witnessed the occurrence. I said I would go immediately to the White House. Stanton told me the President was not there but was at the theatre. "Then," said I, "let us go immediately there."

*The President had been carried across the street from the theatre, to the house of a Mr. Peterson. We entered by ascending a flight of steps above the basement and passing through a long hall to the rear, where the President lay extended on a bed, breathing heavily. Several surgeons were present, at least six, I should think more. Among them I was glad to observe Dr. Hall, who, however, soon left. I inquired of Dr. H., as I entered, the true condition of the President. He replied the President was dead **to all intents**, although he might live three hours or perhaps longer.*

*The giant sufferer lay extended diagonally across the bed, which was not long enough for him. He had been stripped of his clothes. His large arms, which were occasionally exposed, were of a size which one would scarce have expected from his spare appearance. His slow, full **respiration** lifted the clothes with each breath that he took. His features were calm and striking. I had never seen them appear to better advantage than for the first hour, perhaps, that I was there. After that, his right eye began to swell and that part of his face became discolored.*

*Senator [Charles] Sumner was there, I think, when I entered. If not he came in soon after, as did Speaker [of the House Schuyler] Colfax, Mr. Secretary [of the Treasury Hugh] McCulloch, and the other members of the Cabinet, with the exception of Mr. Seward. A double guard was stationed at the door and on the sidewalk, to **repress** the crowd, which was of course highly excited and anxious.*

Admonished: Cautioned or warned.

To all intents: For all practical purposes.

Respiration: Breathing.

Repress: Hold back; restrain.

*The room was small and overcrowded. The surgeons and members of the Cabinet were as many as should have been in the room, but there were many more, and the hall and other rooms in the front or main house were full. One of these rooms was occupied by Mrs. Lincoln and her attendants, with Miss Harris. Mr. Dixon and Mrs. Kinney came to her about twelve o'clock. About once an hour Mrs. Lincoln would **repair** to the bedside of her dying husband and with **lamentation** and tears remain until overcome by emotion.*

*(April 15.) A door which opened upon a porch or gallery, and also the windows, were kept open for fresh air. The night was dark, cloudy, and damp, and about six it began to rain. I remained in the room until then without sitting or leaving it, when, there being a vacant chair which some one left at the foot of the bed, I occupied it for nearly two hours, listening to the heavy groans, and witnessing the wasting life of the good and great man who was **expiring** before me. . . .*

Secretary of State William H. Seward. *(Photograph by Mathew Brady. Courtesy of the Library of Congress.)*

A little before seven, I went into the room where the dying President was rapidly drawing near the closing moments. His wife soon after made her last visit to him. The death-struggle had begun. Robert, his son, stood with several others at the head of the bed. He bore himself well, but on two occasions gave way to overpowering grief and sobbed aloud, turning his head and leaning on the shoulder of Senator Sumner. The respiration of the President became suspended at intervals, and at last entirely ceased at twenty-two minutes past seven. . . .

*I went after breakfast to the Executive Mansion. There was a cheerless cold rain and everything seemed gloomy. On the Avenue in front of the White House were several hundred colored people, mostly women and children, weeping and wailing their loss. This crowd did not appear to diminish through the whole of that cold, wet day; they seemed not to know what was to be their fate since their great **benefactor** was dead, and their hopeless grief affected me more*

Repair: Go.

Lamentation: Expressions of grief.

Expiring: Dying.

Benefactor: Friend or provider of aid.

President Abraham Lincoln's funeral procession travels through New York City.
(Drawing from a photograph by Mathew Brady. From Harper's Weekly.)

than almost anything else, though strong and brave men wept when I met them.

What happened next . . .

Lincoln's death shocked the North out of its celebratory mood and plunged it into one of deep anger and sadness. After all, the Union's victory in the Civil War had made the president very popular across much of the North. Northern communities realized that during the previous four years, Lincoln had managed to keep the dream of a restored Union alive despite many periods of doubt and discouragement. They also knew that victory would not have been possible without his guidance and determination. One Northern

newspaper described the change in mood across the Union by simply stating that "the songs of victory are [now] drowned in sorrow."

The nation entered into a period of mourning in the weeks following Lincoln's death. Thousands of citizens paid their respects to their fallen president when the White House held a service in his honor. On April 20, Lincoln's body was placed on a train so that he could be buried in his hometown of Springfield, Illinois. As Lincoln's funeral car passed through the American countryside during the next few days, millions of farmers and townspeople gathered along the train's route to pay their respects.

In the South, meanwhile, some people were glad to hear of Lincoln's death. But black families were horrified to learn about the assassination, and many white people reacted with sadness as well. Some of these people were simply war-weary citizens who wanted to return to a life of peace. Others

Four of the conspirators involved in President Lincoln's assassination are hanged. *(Courtesy of the Library of Congress.)*

recognized that the assassination might lead the North to treat the South more harshly in the coming months. Confederate president Jefferson Davis (1808–1889), for example, admitted that he had "no special regard for Mr. Lincoln," but stated that "there are a great many men of whose end I had rather hear than his. I fear it will be disastrous to our people, and I regret it deeply."

As Davis suspected, Lincoln's death resulted in a transfer of governmental power to lawmakers who were determined to punish the South for the war and for the death of their president. Vice President Andrew Johnson assumed the presidency after Lincoln's assassination, and both he and leaders in the Republican-controlled Congress indicated that their Reconstruction policies toward the South would be very stern.

The man who assassinated Lincoln, meanwhile, lived for less than two weeks after escaping from Ford's Theatre. Federal soldiers tracked Booth and an accomplice named David Herold to a tobacco barn in Virginia. On April 26, the soldiers surrounded the barn and demanded that the two men surrender. Herold gave himself up, but Booth refused to surrender, and the soldiers set fire to the barn. Booth died of a gunshot wound while still in the burning barn, but it remains uncertain whether the wound was self-inflicted or whether one of the soldiers shot him.

In the weeks following Booth's violent death, eight other alleged participants in the assassination plot were captured and put on trial. All eight were convicted by a military court of being involved in the plan to kill Lincoln, and four of them were hanged. Three others—including Dr. Samuel Mudd (1833-1883), who treated Booth's broken leg several hours after the shooting—were sentenced to life in prison, but they were pardoned (officially forgiven and released from further punishment) in 1869. The eighth person was sentenced to six years in prison for helping Booth get out of Ford's Theatre.

Did you know . . .

- At first, President Johnson and the Republican-controlled Congress seemed to have similar views on Reconstruction. Within a matter of months, however, the relationship between Johnson and Congress deteriorated, as the president resisted legislative efforts to toughen some of his Reconstruction policies. These differences became so great that Congress impeached Johnson (formally accused him of wrongdoing and tried to remove him from office). This effort to get rid of Johnson almost succeeded, but the Senate vote to remove him fell one vote short.

- John Wilkes Booth had an older brother, Edwin Booth (1833–1893), who also made his living as an actor. In fact, many people considered Edwin Booth to be the finest actor of the American theater during the late 1850s and early 1860s. Strongly loyal to the Union, Edwin was very distressed when he learned that his brother had assassinated Lincoln. He spent a year away from the stage following his brother's death, then returned to the theater in 1866. Booth worried that theatergoers might not welcome him back because of his brother's murderous actions, but most audiences accepted him. Edwin Booth continued to make his living as an actor and theatrical manager until 1891, when he retired.

- General Ulysses S. Grant and his wife Julia Dent Grant (1826-1902) were originally supposed to join President Lincoln and the First Lady for the play at Ford's Theatre on the night that the president was shot. But Julia Grant was anxious to visit their children, who were staying in New Jersey. As a result, General Grant politely declined the president's invitation to accompany them to the play, and Mrs. Lincoln invited Major Rathbone and his fiancée instead.

- Today, American presidents are protected by large numbers of agents who are dedicated to defending them from any attack, even if they have to sacrifice their own lives in the process. These protective units were formed to stop tragic incidents like the attack on President Lincoln from ever taking place again. Unfortunately, several presidents were later shot at, including three who died as a result of an assassin's bullet: James A. Garfield (1831–1881), William McKinley (1843–1901), and John F. Kennedy (1917–1963).

- Historians continue to debate various conspiracy theories about the Lincoln assassination today. Some people think that Booth was aided by officials in the Confederate government. Other people have speculated that Booth was helped by officials in the U.S. War Department. Others have charged that Secretary of War Edwin Stanton (1814–1869) took part in the assassination plot because of concerns that Lincoln's Reconstruction policies would not sufficiently punish the South for its wartime actions. Some people have even claimed that Booth escaped from his pursuers, and that the federal agents actually killed a man who only resembled the assassin. But as James M. McPherson noted in *Ordeal by Fire,* "although a number of ambiguities and unanswered questions remain about the assassination, there is no real evidence to support any of these myths. Booth and his handful of accomplices appear to have acted on their own. And indeed, the man killed in Virginia was John Wilkes Booth."

For Further Reading

Harrell, Carolyn L. *When the Bells Tolled for Lincoln.* Macon, GA: Mercer University Press, 1997.

Jakoubek, Robert. *The Assassination of Abraham Lincoln.* Brookfield, CT: Millbrook Press, 1993.

January, Brendan. *The Assassination of Abraham Lincoln.* New York: Children's Press, 1998.

Lloyd, Lewis. *The Assassination of Lincoln: History and Myth.* Lincoln: University of Nebraska Press, 1994.

Nash, Thomas P., Jr. *A Naval History of the Civil War.* South Brunswick, NJ: A. S. Barnes, 1972.

Oates, Stephen B. *With Malice Toward None: The Life of Abraham Lincoln.* New York: Harper & Row, 1977. Reprint, New York: HarperPerennial, 1994.

Henry McNeal Turner

14

Excerpt from "I Claim the Rights of a Man"
Speech before the Georgia State Legislature, September 3, 1868

An expelled black senator defends his right to hold office

The North's victory in the Civil War in 1865 settled two important issues. First, it established that states were not allowed to leave, or secede from, the United States. Second, it put an end to slavery throughout the country. But the end of the war also raised a whole new set of issues. For example, federal lawmakers had to decide whether to punish the Confederate leaders for their rebellion. They also had to decide what process to use to readmit the Southern states to the Union, and how much assistance to provide in securing equal rights for the freed slaves. The period in American history immediately after the Civil War—when the country struggled to deal with these important and complicated issues—was called Reconstruction.

Reconstruction was a time of great political and social turmoil. President Andrew Johnson (1808–1875), who took office after Abraham Lincoln (1809–1865) was assassinated in 1865, controlled the earliest Reconstruction efforts. Johnson said that the Southern states could form new state governments and be readmitted to the Union once they abolished (put an end to) slavery and admitted that they had been

> "God saw fit to vary everything in nature. There are no two men alike—no two voices alike—no two trees alike. God has weaved and tissued variety and versatility throughout the boundless space of His creation. Because God saw fit to make some red, and some white, and some black, and some brown, are we to sit here in judgment upon what God has seen fit to do?"

wrong to secede. He also pardoned (officially forgave) many men who had held important positions in the Confederate government or army.

Within a short time, however, many Northerners came to believe that Johnson's Reconstruction policies were too lenient (easy) on the South. They worried that the same men who had led the Southern states to secede from the Union would return to power. In December 1865, for example, the people of Georgia elected former Confederate vice president Andrew Stephens to represent them in the U.S. Congress. Other Southern states elected former Confederate politicians and military leaders to public office as well.

As state legislatures re-formed across the South, it became clear that the former Confederate states had no intention of giving black people equal rights as citizens. Instead, most Southern states passed laws known as "Black Codes" to regulate the behavior of blacks and make sure that whites maintained control over them. The state of Georgia not only instituted Black Codes but also rejected the Fourteenth Amendment, which made black people citizens of the United States and granted them civil rights.

In response to such actions by the Southern states, the U.S. Congress decided to take over the process of Reconstruction from the president. Beginning in 1866, Congress enacted stricter Reconstruction policies and sent in federal troops to enforce them. Political leaders in Georgia were determined to avoid complying with (following) these policies. They asked the U.S. Supreme Court to issue an injunction (a court order preventing a law from being enforced), but their case was dismissed.

Congress's Reconstruction policies required the Southern states to hold conventions to rewrite their constitutions. Georgia's constitutional convention met in Atlanta in December 1867. Of the 169 delegates (elected representatives) at the convention, 37 were black men. "The convention was interested in suffrage [voting rights], qualifications for office-holding, relief [aid to the poor], and a liberal Constitution," according to W. E. B. DuBois in *Black Reconstruction*. "In these matters, Negroes took active part in the discussions, and used their political privilege intelligently, and with caution." The delegates created a new state constitution that prohibited slavery and granted all adult males—black and white—the right to vote. However, it did not specifically say that all legal voters would be eligible to hold public office.

Once Georgia and the other Southern states had developed new constitutions, they were allowed to elect state governments and rejoin the Union. A majority of Georgia voters approved the new state constitution in April 1868. They also elected new representatives to the state and federal governments. Many black men jumped at the chance to vote and have a say in their government. As a result, the new Georgia State Senate included three black members, while the State House of Representatives included twenty-nine black members.

The U.S. Congress welcomed Georgia back into the Union on July 21, 1868, shortly after the state ratified (approved) the Fourteenth Amendment. Then Congress withdrew the federal troops that had been sent to enforce their Reconstruction policies. But as soon as the federal troops left Georgia, the white majority in the state legislature began trying to expel (kick out) the black members because of their race. "Immediately upon the readmission of their states the Conservatives [people who want to maintain traditional, established views or conditions] . . . began their running attack on the new administrations," John Hope Franklin wrote in *Reconstruction after the Civil War*. "Overthrow would come soon, they felt, if they worked hard enough at it."

In the Georgia State Senate, white members of the Democratic Party began targeting black members of the Republican Party. They accused the three black senators of "gross insults" and other minor offenses. But even though the charges were ridiculous, the Democrats held a majority in the senate and had enough votes to expel the black members. In September 1868, the white members of the Georgia State House of Representatives passed a resolution (a formal expression of their opinion) stating that black men were not eligible to hold public office. They argued that the state constitution allowed blacks to vote, but did not allow them to hold office. Based upon this resolution, twenty-five of the twenty-nine black state representatives lost their seats in the House. They were replaced by white Democrats. The other four black

Henry McNeal Turner

Henry McNeal Turner was born in Columbia, South Carolina, in 1834, to free black parents. (Not all black people in the United States were slaves in the early 1800s. Some former slaves were set free when their white owners died or no longer needed their services. Other former slaves saved money and purchased their freedom from their owners. When free blacks had children, the children were also free.) Even though Turner was free from birth, he still spent some time working alongside slaves on a cotton-growing plantation as a boy.

In 1855, Turner moved to Macon, Georgia. He joined the African Methodist Episcopal Church and became a preacher. His sermons attracted the attention of white people in Georgia. Many white people resented blacks who knew how to read and write, because they worried that educated blacks would encourage slaves to

rebel against their masters. As a result, fearful whites pressured Turner to leave Georgia. He moved north to Washington, D.C., where he became pastor of Israel Bethel Church. Over the next few years, he emerged as a leader of the black community and a fighter for racial justice.

In 1863, President Abraham Lincoln appointed Turner to be chaplain for the first black troops who fought for the United States in the Civil War. When the war ended in 1865, Turner took a job in the Freedmen's Bureau, a federal government agency organized to help former slaves make the transition to freedom. He traveled around Georgia speaking to freed slaves about education and job opportunities. By 1867, when the U.S. Congress took control of Reconstruction, Turner was a prominent figure in Georgia politics.

members remained in office because they had such light skin that it was impossible to prove their race.

Henry McNeal Turner (1834–1915) was one of the black men expelled from the Georgia legislature. He was an educated man and a respected minister, but his status as a leader in the black community made him one of the primary targets of racist white Democrats. Turner refused to accept the ruling of his colleagues. On September 3, 1868, he made a passionate speech before the Georgia House of Representatives defending his right to hold office. The legislature refused to print the text of his speech in its minutes (the official written record of a meeting), so Turner published it himself and distributed it among the people of Georgia.

Henry McNeal Turner. *(Reproduced by permission of Fisk University Library.)*

lasting changes to Georgia society. The following year, he was elected to serve in the Georgia House of Representatives. But in September 1868, the conservative white members of the Congress voted to expel all of the black representatives. Turner led the protests against this decision and even went to Washington to make a formal complaint to the U.S. Congress. He and the other black representatives finally regained their seats in 1870.

Turner's experiences in Georgia during Reconstruction convinced him that Southern whites would never allow blacks to be equal members of society. He then began supporting the idea that black Americans should migrate to Africa and form their own country. Turner was ordained a bishop in the African Methodist Episcopal Church in 1880. He died in Windsor, Ontario, Canada, in 1915.

Turner took part in the convention to rewrite the Georgia State Constitution in 1867. He stressed the importance of compromising with whites in order to make

Things to remember while reading the excerpt from Henry McNeal Turner's speech before the Georgia State Legislature:

- Turner argues that he has a right to hold office in the new state government because that government was set up by blacks. Black delegates played an active role in the convention that rewrote Georgia's constitution. In addition, black voters selected him and the other black members of the legislature to be their representatives. He claims that black politicians are more capable of representing the will of the black people of Georgia than white politicians could be.

- One of the most difficult issues following the end of the Civil War involved helping former slaves build new, independent lives for themselves. To many former slaves, true freedom meant owning land of their own. This way they could grow crops to feed their families and would no longer be dependent on plantation owners. Some people in the North wanted the U.S. government to confiscate (take away) land belonging to Southerners who had supported the Confederacy and give it to former slaves and poor whites. But other people did not want to give the government the right to take away citizens' property. President Johnson dashed the hopes of many former slaves to own land when he issued pardons to numerous former Confederates. People who received a pardon got back their rights and their property. In the end, the U.S. government failed to provide land to most former slaves. Turner refers to this situation in his speech. "You have our land and your own too," he tells the white legislators. "We [black people], who number hundreds of thousands in Georgia, including our wives and families, [have] not a foot of land to call our own."

- At one point in his speech, Turner remarks that he has tried so hard to get along with white politicians that "many among my own party have classed me as a Democrat." In fact, Turner and most black people in the United States felt strong ties to the Republican political party during Reconstruction. They associated the Republican Party with President Abraham Lincoln, the end of slavery in the United States, and an increase in black civil rights and political power. Black voters tended to support Republican candidates for the next sixty years. But this situation began to change during the Great Depression of the 1930s. At that time, Democratic president Franklin D. Roosevelt (1882–1945) established programs to provide jobs and other forms of assistance to black families. Then, during the civil rights movement of the 1960s, President Lyndon B. Johnson (1908–1973) and the Democratic Congress passed sweeping new laws that protected and expanded the civil rights of black Americans. By the 1990s, most black voters tended to support Democratic candidates.

Excerpt from "I Claim the Rights of a Man," Henry McNeal Turner's speech before the Georgia State Legislature:

*Mr. Speaker: Before proceeding to argue this question upon its **intrinsic** merits, I wish the members of this House to understand the position that I take. I hold that I am a member of this **body**. Therefore, sir, I shall neither **fawn** nor **cringe** before any party, nor stoop to beg them for my rights. Some of my colored fellow members, in the course of their remarks, took occasion to appeal to the sympathies of members on the opposite side, and to **eulogize** their character for **magnanimity**. It reminds me very much, sir, of slaves begging under the lash. I am here to demand my rights and to hurl thunderbolts at the men who would dare to cross the threshold of my manhood. There is an old **aphorism** which says, "fight the devil with fire," and if I should observe the rule in this instance, I wish gentlemen to understand that it is but fighting them with their own weapon.*

*The scene presented in this House, today, is one **unparalleled** in the history of the world. From this day, back to the day when God breathed the breath of life into **Adam**, no **analogy** for it can be found. Never, in the history of the world, has a man been **arraigned** before a body **clothed** with legislative, judicial or executive functions, charged with the offense of being a darker **hue** than his fellow men. I know that questions have been before the courts of this country, and of other countries, involving topics not altogether dissimilar to that which is being discussed here today. But, sir, never in the history of the great nations of this world—never before—has a man been arraigned, charged with an offense committed by the God of Heaven Himself. Cases may be found where men have been **deprived** of their rights for crimes and **misdemeanors**; but it has remained for the state of Georgia, in the very heart of the nineteenth century, to call a man before the **bar,** and there charge him with an act for which he is no more responsible than for the head which he carries upon his shoulders. The **Anglo-Saxon** race, sir, is a most surprising one. No man has ever been more deceived in that race than I have been for the last three weeks. I was not aware that there was in the character of that race so much cowardice or so much **pusillanimity**. The **treachery** which has been exhibited in it by gentlemen belonging to*

Intrinsic: Basic or underlying.

Body: Group of individuals organized for a certain purpose (in this case, the Georgia State House of Representatives).

Fawn: Flatter or show affection in order to gain favor.

Cringe: Behave in a submissive way.

Eulogize: Speak about with high praise.

Magnanimity: Showing a generous spirit.

Aphorism: Saying.

Unparalleled: Without equal.

Adam: The first man created by God, according to the Bible.

Analogy: Similar or corresponding situation.

Arraigned: Charged with wrongdoing.

Clothed: Powered.

Hue: Shade or color.

Deprived: Taken away or withheld.

Misdemeanors: Less serious crimes.

Bar: Court system.

Anglo-Saxon: White people of English background.

Pusillanimity: Extreme timidity or cowardliness.

Treachery: Deception or betrayal of trust.

that race has shaken my confidence in it more than anything that has come under my observation from the day of my birth. . . .

*Whose legislature is this? Is it a white man's legislature, or is it a black man's legislature? Who voted for a constitutional convention, in obedience to the **mandate** of the Congress of the United States? Who first rallied around the standard of Reconstruction? Who set the ball of loyalty rolling in the state of Georgia? And whose voice was heard on the hills and in the valleys of this state? It was the voice of the brawny-armed Negro, with the few **humanitarian-hearted** white men who came to our assistance. I claim the honor, sir, of having been the instrument of convincing hundreds—yea, thousands—of white men, that to reconstruct under the **measures** of the United States Congress was the safest and the best course for the interest of the state.*

*Let us look at some facts in connection with this matter. Did half the white men of Georgia vote for this legislature? Did not the great bulk of them fight, with all their strength, the **Constitution** under which we are acting? And did they not fight against the organization of this legislature? And further, sir, did they not vote against it? Yes, sir! And there are persons in this legislature today who are ready to spit their poison in my face, while they themselves opposed, with all their power, the **ratification** of this Constitution. They question my right to sit in this body, to represent the people whose legal votes elected me. This objection, sir, is an unheard-of **monopoly** of power. No analogy can be found for it, except it be the case of a man who should go into my house, take possession of my wife and children, and then tell me to walk out. I stand very much in the position of a criminal before your bar, because I dare to be the **exponent** of the views of those who sent me here. Or, in other words, we are told that if black men want to speak, they must speak through white **trumpets**; if black men want their sentiments expressed, they must be **adulterated** and sent through white messengers, who will **quibble** and **equivocate** and evade as rapidly as the **pendulum** of a clock. If this be not done, then the black men have committed an outrage, and their representatives must be denied the right to represent their **constituents**.*

The great question, sir, is this: Am I a man? If I am such, I claim the rights of a man. Am I not a man because I happen to be of a darker hue than honorable gentlemen around me? Let me see whether I am or not. I want to convince the House today that I am entitled to my seat here. . . . Am I a man? Have I a soul to save, as

Mandate: Formal order.

Humanitarian-hearted: People who promote social reform and the welfare of others.

Measures: Proposed legal steps.

Constitution: The new Georgia State Constitution prepared during Reconstruction.

Ratification: Approval.

Monopoly: Complete control.

Exponent: Person who argues in favor of something; advocate.

Trumpets: Funnel-shaped devices for directing sound.

Adulterated: Corrupted or tainted.

Quibble: Argue about minor issues; bicker.

Equivocate: Mislead or deceive.

Pendulum: A device that swings freely back and forth.

Constituents: A group that elects a person to public office.

you have? Am I **susceptible** of **eternal development**, as you are? Can I learn all the arts and sciences that you can? Has it ever been demonstrated in the history of the world? Have black men ever exhibited bravery as white men have done? Have they ever been in the **professions?** Have they not as good **articulative organs** as you? . . . God saw fit to vary everything in nature. There are no two men alike—no two voices alike—no two trees alike. God has weaved and **tissued** variety and versatility throughout the boundless space of His creation. Because God saw fit to make some red, and some white, and some black, and some brown, are we to sit here in judgment upon what God has seen fit to do? As well might one play with the thunderbolts of heaven as with that creature that bears God's image—God's photograph. . . .

If I am not permitted to occupy a seat here, for the purpose of representing my constituents, I want to know how white men can be permitted to do so. How can a white man represent a colored **constituency,** if a colored man cannot do it? The great argument is: "Oh, we have **inherited**" this, that and the other. Now, I want gentlemen to come down to cool, common sense. Is the created greater than the Creator? Is man greater than God? It is very strange, if a white man can occupy on this floor a seat created by colored votes, and a black man cannot do it. Why, gentlemen, it is the most **shortsighted** reasoning in the world. . . .

It is said that Congress never gave us the right to hold office. I want to know, sir, if the Reconstruction measures did not base their action on the ground that no **distinction** should be made on account of race, color or **previous condition?** Was not that the grand **fulcrum** on which they rested? And did not every reconstructed state have to reconstruct on the idea that no discrimination, in any sense of the term, should be made? There is not a man here who will dare say No. If Congress has simply given me merely sufficient civil and political rights to make me a mere political slave for Democrats, or anybody else—giving them the opportunity of jumping on my back in order to leap into political power—I do not thank Congress for it. Never, so help me God, shall I be a political slave. I am not now speaking for those colored men who sit with me in this House, nor do I say that they **endorse** my sentiments, but assisting Mr. Lincoln to take me out of **servile** slavery did not intend to put me and my race into political slavery. If they did, let them take away my **ballot**—I do not want it, and shall not have it. I don't want to be a mere tool of that sort. I have been a slave long enough already.

Susceptible: Capable.

Eternal development: Continued growth and a lasting relationship with God.

Professions: Jobs requiring special knowledge, such as medicine and law.

Articulative organs: Parts of the body used in speaking, including the mouth and throat.

Tissued: Covered with cellular material.

Constituency: A group of citizens who elect a representative to government.

Inherited: Receive as a right from ancestors.

Shortsighted: Without thinking about the future.

Distinction: Difference.

Previous condition: Having once been a slave.

Fulcrum: Support.

Endorse: Approve publicly.

Servile: Demeaning or submissive.

Ballot: Right to vote.

Submitted: Presented for review.

Constitutional Amendment: The Fourteenth Amendment, which made black people citizens of the United States and granted them basic civil rights.

Resolution: Formal expression of the opinion or intent of a group.

Proposition: Proposal or suggestion.

Abide: Accept without objection.

Rhetorical: Relating to speech.

Eloquence: Speaking in a forceful or expressive manner.

Derision: Contempt.

Endeavored: Attempted or tried.

Overseer: The person in charge of field hands on a plantation.

Conservative: Traditional; tending to support existing conditions or established views.

Adhered: Stuck.

Thrust: Attack.

*I tell you what I would be willing to do: I am willing that the question should be **submitted** to Congress for an explanation as to what was meant in the passage of their Reconstruction measures, and of the **Constitutional Amendment**. Let the Democratic party in this House pass a **resolution** giving this subject that direction, and I shall be content. I dare you, gentlemen, to do it. Come up to the question openly, whether it meant that the Negro might hold office, or whether it meant that he should merely have the right to vote. If you are honest men, you will do it. If, however, you will not do that, I would make another **proposition**: Call together, again, the convention that framed the constitution under which we are acting; let them take a vote upon the subject, and I am willing to **abide** by their decision. . . .*

*These colored men, who are unable to express themselves with all the clearness and dignity and force of **rhetorical eloquence**, are laughed at in **derision** by the Democracy of the country. It reminds me very much of the man who looked at himself in a mirror and, imagining that he was addressing another person, exclaimed: "My God, how ugly you are!" These gentlemen do not consider for a moment the dreadful hardships which these people have endured, and especially those who in any way **endeavored** to acquire an education. For myself, sir, I was raised in the cotton field of South Carolina, and in order to prepare myself for usefulness, as well to myself as to my race, I determined to devote my spare hours to study. When the **overseer** retired at night to his comfortable couch, I sat and read and thought and studied, until I heard him blow his horn in the morning. He frequently told me, with an oath, that if he discovered me attempting to learn, that he would whip me to death, and I have no doubt he would have done so, if he had found an opportunity. I prayed to Almighty God to assist me, and He did, and I thank Him with my whole heart and soul. . . .*

*So far as I am personally concerned, no man in Georgia has been more **conservative** than I. "Anything to please the white folks" has been my motto; and so closely have I **adhered** to that course, that many among my own party have classed me as a Democrat. One of the leaders of the Republican party in Georgia has not been at all favorable to me for some time back, because he believed that I was too "conservative" for a Republican. I can assure you, however, Mr. Speaker, that I have had quite enough, and to spare, of such "conservatism". . . .*

*But, Mr. Speaker, I do not regard this movement as a **thrust** at me. It is a thrust at the Bible—a thrust at the God of the Universe, for* making a man and not finishing him; it is simply calling the **Great Jehovah** a fool. Why, sir, though we are not white, we have accomplished much. We have **pioneered** civilization here; we have built up your country; we have worked in your fields and **garnered** your harvests for two hundred and fifty years! And what do we ask in return? Do we ask you for **compensation** for the sweat our fathers bore for you—for the tears you have caused, and the hearts you have broken, and the lives you have **curtailed**, and the blood you have spilled? Do we ask **retaliation?** We ask it not. We are willing to let the dead past bury its dead; but we ask you, now for our rights. You have all the elements of superiority upon your side; you have our money and your own; you have our education and your own; and you have our land and your own too. We, who number hundreds of thousands in Georgia, including our wives and families, with not a foot of land to call our own—strangers in the land of our birth; without money, without education, without aid, without a roof to cover us while we live, nor sufficient clay to cover us when we die! It is extraordinary that a race such as yours, professing **gallantry** and **chivalry** and education and superiority, living in a land where ringing chimes call child and **sire** to the church of God—a land where Bibles are read and Gospel truths are spoken, and where courts of justice are **presumed** to exist; that with all these advantages on your side, you can make war upon the poor defenseless black man. You know we have no money, no railroads, no telegraphs, no advantages of any sort, and yet all manner of **injustice** is placed upon us. You know that the black people of this country acknowledge you as their superiors, by virtue of your education and advantages. . . .

You may **expel** us, gentlemen, but I firmly believe that you will some day **repent** it. . . . Every act that we commit is like a bounding ball. If you curse a man, that curse rebounds upon you; and when you bless a man, the blessing returns to you; and when you **oppress** a man, the oppression also will rebound. Where have you ever heard of four millions of freemen being governed by laws, and yet have no **hand** in their making? Search the records of the world, and you will find no example. "Governments derive their just powers from the consent of the governed." How dare you to make laws by which to try me and my wife and children, and deny me a voice in the making of these laws? . . . How can you say that you have a **republican** form of government, when you make such distinction and enact such **proscriptive** laws? . . .

We are a **persecuted** people. . . . Good men in all nations have been persecuted; but the persecutors have been handed down to

Great Jehovah: God.

Pioneered: Created or originated.

Garnered: Collected.

Compensation: Payment.

Curtailed: Cut short.

Retaliation: Revenge or repayment.

Gallantry: Brave and courteous conduct.

Chivalry: Honorable and generous conduct.

Sire: Father

Presumed: Understood or assumed.

Injustice: Unfair violation of rights.

Expel: Force to leave.

Repent: Regret.

Oppress: Hold down or burden through abuse of power.

Hand: Involvement.

Republican: A type of government in which citizens hold the power and vote to elect representatives.

Proscriptive: Harshly restrictive.

Persecuted: Harassed or caused to suffer harm because of differences.

posterity with shame and *ignominy*. If you pass this bill, you will never get Congress to *pardon* or *enfranchise* another *rebel* in your lives. You are going to fix an everlasting *disfranchisement* upon *Mr. Toombs* and the other leading men of Georgia. You may think you are doing yourselves honor by expelling us from this House, but when we go . . . we will light a torch of truth that will never be extinguished—the *impression* that will run through the country, as people picture in their mind's eye these poor black men, in all parts of this Southern country, pleading for their rights. When you expel us, you make us forever your political *foes*, and you will never find a black man to vote a Democratic *ticket* again; for, so help me God, I will go through all the length and breadth of the land, where a man of my race is to be found, and advise him to beware of the Democratic party. Justice is the great *doctrine* taught in the Bible. God's Eternal Justice is founded upon Truth, and the man who steps from Justice steps from Truth, and cannot make his principles to *prevail*. . . .

*You may expel us, gentlemen, by your votes, today; but, while you do it, remember that there is a just God in Heaven, whose All-Seeing Eye beholds alike the acts of the oppressor and the oppressed, and who, despite the *machinations* of the wicked, never fails to *vindicate* the cause of Justice, and the *sanctity* of His own handiwork.*

What happened next . . .

Shortly after Turner and the other black representatives were expelled from the Georgia legislature, the remaining Republican members asked the Georgia Supreme Court to decide whether blacks were eligible to hold public office under the constitution. The Supreme Court said that blacks were entitled to hold office. But the state legislature refused to accept the court's decision. In October 1868, Turner and several other black legislators protested to the U.S. Congress's Committee on Reconstruction. They claimed that the Georgia state legislature was illegal because it had not been formed under Congress's Reconstruction policies. The committee conducted an investigation and learned of widespread violations of black people's rights in Georgia.

Posterity: Future generations.

Ignominy: Personal disgrace or humiliation.

Pardon: Officially forgive.

Enfranchise: Grant the right to vote.

Rebel: Confederate.

Disfranchisement: Denial of the right to vote.

Mr. Toombs: Robert A. Toombs (1810–1885), who acted as secretary of state in the Confederacy and lost his right to vote under Reconstruction.

Impression: Image or idea.

Foes: Opponents or enemies.

Ticket: List of candidates for election.

Doctrine: Basic principle.

Prevail: Triumph.

Machinations: Tricky or deceitful actions.

Vindicate: Justify or prove correct.

Sanctity: Holiness or sacredness.

In December 1868, the U.S. Congress refused to allow the men who had been elected to represent Georgia in the federal government to take their seats. Since Georgia had no representation in the U.S. government, the state was still not technically part of the Union. But this action did not convince the state legislature to readmit its black members. The last straw came in March 1869, when Georgia failed to ratify the Fifteenth Amendment to the U.S. Constitution. This amendment guaranteed black voting rights and prohibited the states from restricting them. When Georgia rejected the Fifteenth Amendment, the U.S. Congress sent federal troops into the state again. Congress declared that it would not readmit Georgia to the Union until the state ratified the amendment and allowed the black members to return to the state legislature.

General Alfred H. Terry (1827–1890) took over control of Georgia's state government. He expelled a number of white Democrats from the state legislature and allowed Turner and

The Ku Klux Klan was the most notable white supremacist group to form in the years following the Civil War.

the other black representatives to return to office. This new Georgia legislature ratified the Fifteenth Amendment and formally recognized the right of black men to hold public office in the state. It also voted to pay the black legislators for the time they were not allowed to serve. On January 10, 1870, Georgia was readmitted to the Union for a second time.

Did you know . . .

- The situation in the Georgia state legislature was only one example of continuing racism in the South after the Civil War ended. Anger over Congress's Reconstruction policies convinced many white Southerners to use any means necessary to reclaim control of their governments and society. Some people—known as "white supremacists" due to their belief that blacks were inferior—used violence and terrorism to intimidate blacks and any whites who helped them. One of the worst white supremacist groups was the Ku Klux Klan, which was formed in 1866. Members of the Klan and similar groups bombed or set fire to black schools and churches. They terrorized black officeholders, successful black farmers and businessmen, and white teachers who worked at black schools. They were rarely punished for these crimes because juries were afraid to convict them. As a result of their activities, many blacks were too intimidated to vote and political leadership in the South gradually returned to the hands of whites.

For Further Reading

DuBois, W. E. B. *Black Reconstruction.* New York: Harcourt, 1935. Reprint, New York: Atheneum, 1992.

Foner, Eric. *Reconstruction: America's Unfinished Revolution, 1863–1877.* New York: Harper and Row, 1988.

Foner, Philip S., and Robert James Branham, eds. *Lift Every Voice: African American Oratory, 1787–1900.* Tuscaloosa: University of Alabama Press, 1998.

Franklin, John Hope. *Reconstruction after the Civil War.* Chicago: University of Chicago Press, 1961, 1994.

Where to Learn More

The following list of resources focuses on material appropriate for middle school or high school students. Please note that the web site addresses were verified prior to publication, but are subject to change.

Books

Anders, Curt. *Hearts in Conflict: A One-Volume History of the Civil War.* Secaucus, NJ: Carol Pub. Group, 1994.

Anderson, Nancy Scott, and Dwight Anderson. *The Generals—Ulysses S. Grant and Robert E. Lee.* New York: Knopf, 1988.

Aptheker, Herbert. *Abolitionism: A Revolutionary Movement.* Boston: Twayne, 1989.

Basler, Roy P., ed. *The Collected Works of Abraham Lincoln.* New Brunswick, NJ: Rutgers University Press, 1953.

Berlin, Ira, Joseph P. Reidy, and Leslie S. Rowland, eds. *Freedom's Soldiers: The Black Military Experience in the Civil War.* New York: Cambridge University Press, 1998.

Blight, David W. *Frederick Douglass's Civil War: Keeping Faith in Jubilee.* Baton Rouge: Louisiana State University Press, 1989.

Bradford, Ned, ed. *Battles and Leaders of the Civil War.* New York: New American Library, 1984.

Buell, Thomas B. *The Warrior Generals: Combat Leadership in the Civil War.* New York: Crown, 1997.

Carter, Alden R. *The Civil War: American Tragedy.* New York: Franklin Watts, 1992.

Carter, Samuel. *The Last Cavaliers: Confederate and Union Cavalry in the Civil War.* St. Martin's Press, 1980.

Catton, Bruce. *The Centennial History of the Civil War.* 3 vols. Garden City, NY: Doubleday, 1961–65.

Catton, Bruce. *The Civil War.* Boston: Houghton Mifflin, 1960.

Chadwick, Bruce. *The Two American Presidents: A Dual Biography of Abraham Lincoln and Jefferson Davis.* Secaucus, NJ: Carol, 1999.

Chang, Ina. *A Separate Battle: Women and the Civil War.* New York: Scholastic, 1994.

Civil War Generals: An Illustrated Encyclopedia. New York: Gramercy, 1999.

Commager, Henry Steele. *The Blue and the Gray.* Indianapolis: Bobbs-Merrill, 1950.

Davis, William C. *The Commanders of the Civil War.* San Diego: Thunder Bay Press, 1999.

Davis, William C. *Jefferson Davis: The Man and His Hour.* New York: HarperCollins, 1991.

Donald, David Herbert. *Lincoln.* New York: Simon & Schuster, 1995.

Dowdey, Clifford. *Lee's Last Campaign: The Story of Lee and His Men against Grant.* Lincoln: University of Nebraska Press, 1993.

Foote, Shelby. *The Civil War: A Narrative.* 3 vols. New York: Random House, 1958–74.

Freeman, Douglas S. *Lee's Lieutenants.* 3 vols. New York: Scribner's, 1942–44.

Goen, C. C. *Broken Churches, Broken Nation.* Macon, GA: Mercer University Press, 1985.

Grant, Ulysses S. *Personal Memoirs of U. S. Grant.* New York: Library of America, 1990.

Green, Carl R., and William R. Sanford. *Confederate Generals of the Civil War.* Springfield, NJ: Enslow, 1998.

Green, Carl R., and William R. Sanford. *Union Generals of the Civil War.* Springfield, NJ: Enslow, 1998.

Grimsley, Mark. *The Hard Hand of War, Union Military Policy Toward Southern Civilians, 1861–1865.* New York: Cambridge University Press, 1995.

Gutman, Herbert G. *The Black Family in Slavery and Freedom.* New York: Pantheon, 1976.

Hargrove, Hondon B. *Black Union Soldiers in the Civil War.* Jefferson, NC: McFarland, 1988.

Harmon, Dan. *Civil War Generals.* Philadelphia: Chelsea House, 1997.

Harrell, Carolyn L. *When the Bells Tolled for Lincoln*. Macon, GA: Mercer University Press, 1997.

Haskins, J. *The Day Fort Sumter Was Fired On: A Photo History of the Civil War*. New York: Scholastic, 1995.

Hattaway, Herman. *Shades of Blue and Gray: An Introductory Military History of the Civil War*. Columbia: University of Missouri Press, 1997.

Hendrickson, Robert. *The Road to Appomattox*. New York: John Wiley & Sons, 1998.

Hennessey, John. *Return to Bull Run: The Campaign and Battle of Second Manassas*. New York: Simon & Schuster, 1992.

Holt, Michael F. *The Political Crisis of the 1850s*. New York: John Wiley & Sons, 1978.

Kunhardt, Philip B., Jr. *A New Birth of Freedom: Lincoln at Gettysburg*. Boston: Little, Brown, 1983.

Leonard, Elizabeth D. *All the Daring of the Soldier: Women of the Civil War Armies*. New York: W. W. Norton, 1999.

Lincoln, Abraham. *Abraham Lincoln: Speeches and Writings*. 2 vols. New York: Library of America, 1989.

Linderman, Gerald. *Embattled Courage: The Experience of Combat in the American Civil War*. New York: Free Press, 1987.

Litwack, Leon. *Been in the Storm So Long: The Aftermath of Slavery*. New York: Alfred A. Knopf, 1979.

Macdonald, John. *Great Battles of the Civil War*. New York: Macmillan, 1988.

Macmillan Encylopedia of the Confederacy. New York: Macmillan, 1998.

Massey, Mary Elizabeth. *Women in the Civil War*. Lincoln: University of Nebraska Press, 1966.

McFeely, William S. *Grant: A Biography*. New York: Norton, 1981.

McPherson, James M. *Battle Cry of Freedom*. New York: Oxford University Press, 1988.

McPherson, James M. *For Cause and Comrades: Why Men Fought in the Civil War*. New York: Oxford University Press, 1997.

McPherson, James M. *Ordeal by Fire: The Civil War and Reconstruction*. New York: Alfred A. Knopf, 1982.

McPherson, James M., ed. *Encyclopedia of Civil War Biographies*. Armonk, NY: Sharpe Reference, 2000.

Mitchell, Joseph B. *Military Leaders in the Civil War*. New York: Putnam, 1972.

Mitchell, Reid. *Civil War Soldiers: Their Expectations and Their Experiences*. New York: Viking, 1988.

Morris, Roy, Jr. *Sheridan: The Life and Wars of General Phil Sheridan*. New York: Crown, 1992.

Murphy, Jim. *The Long Road to Gettysburg*. New York: Scholastic, 1995.

Nolan, Alan T. *Lee Considered: General Robert E. Lee and Civil War History*. Chapel Hill: University of North Carolina Press, 1991.

Oates, Stephen B. *With Malice Toward None: The Life of Abraham Lincoln*. New York: Harper & Row, 1977.

Paludan, Phillip S. *The Presidency of Abraham Lincoln*. Lawrence: University Press of Kansas, 1994.

Potter, David M. *The Impending Crisis, 1848–1861*. New York: Harper & Row, 1976.

Ritter, Charles F., and Jon L. Wakelyn. *Leaders of the American Civil War*. Westport, CT: Greenwood Press, 1998.

Royster, Charles. *The Destructive War: William Tecumseh Sherman, Stonewall Jackson, and the Americans*. New York: Alfred A. Knopf, 1991.

Sandburg, Carl. *Abraham Lincoln: The War Years*. 4 vols. New York: Harcourt Brace, 1939.

Sifakis, Stewart. *Who Was Who in the Civil War*. New York: Facts on File, 1988.

Stewart, James Brewer. *Holy Warriors: The Abolitionists and American Slavery*. New York: Hill & Wang, 1976.

Stokesbury, James L. *A Short History of the Civil War*. New York: William Morrow, 1995.

Thomas, Emory. *The Confederate Nation, 1861–1865*. New York: Harper & Row, 1979.

Tracey, Patrick Austin. *Military Leaders of the Civil War*. New York: Facts on File, 1993.

Trelease, Allen W. *Reconstruction: The Great Experiment*. New York: Harper & Row, 1971.

Trudeau, Noah Andre. *Like Men of War: Black Troops in the Civil War, 1862–1865*. Boston: Little, Brown, 1998.

Venet, Wendy Hamand. *Neither Ballots Nor Bullets: Women Abolitionists and the Civil War*. Charlottesville: University Press of Virginia, 1991.

Ward, Geoffrey C. *The Civil War: An Illustrated History*. New York: Alfred A. Knopf, 1990.

Woodworth, Steven E. *Jefferson Davis and His Generals*. Lawrence: University Press of Kansas, 1990.

World Wide Web

American Civil War/Conflict Between the States. http://americanhistory.miningco.com/education/history/americanhistory/msub13.htm (accessed on October 20, 1999).

American Civil War Homepage. http://sunsite.utk.edu/civil-war (accessed on October 20, 1999).

American Civil War Resources on the Internet. http://www.janke.washcoll. edu/civilwar/civilwar.htm (accessed on October 20, 1999).

Civil War Music and Poetry and Music of the War Between the States. http:// users.erols.com/kfraser/ (accessed on October 20, 1999).

Library of Congress. *Gettysburg Address Exhibit.* www.lcweb.loc.gov/ exhibits/gadd (accessed on October 20, 1999).

Library of Congress, American Memory. *Selected Civil War Photographs.* lcweb2.loc.gov/ammem/cwphome.html (accessed on October 20, 1999).

Rutgers University Libraries. *Civil War Resources on the Internet.* http:// www.libraries.rutgers.edu/rulib/socsci/hist/civwar-2.html (accessed on October 20, 1999).

Index

Note: Illustrations are indicated by (ill.)